№ 19

G | W | Y | N | N

| A TRIBUTE TO THE CAREER OF MR. PADRE

Gwynn: A Tribute to The Career of Mr. Padre

Published in the United States of America
by Word Smith Media Ventures, LLC
3600 Clipper Mill Road, Suite 155
Baltimore, MD 21211

ISBN 978-0-9791975-1-2

ACKNOWLEDGEMENTS: Cover design and art direction by Brad Meerholz. Graphic design and layout by Kimberly Shilling. Special projects editor, Jennifer Nelson. Printed by Whitmore Group.

SPECIAL THANKS: Stan Charles, Larry Harris, Kevin Heitz, Staci Wolfson, John Coulson, Rick Marsalek, Tyler Covahey, Mark Luterman, John Boggs, Bob Chandler, Jim Henneman, Steve Giles, Marvin Milstein and Jay Strecker.

PHOTOGRAPHY: Andy Hayt/MLB Photos/Getty Images: Cover. Jon SooHoo/MLB Photos/Getty Images: 5. Diamond Images/ Getty Images: 7. Stephen Dunn/Getty Images: 9, 24, 59. San Diego State University Athletics: 13, 14, 42, 44, 55, 57. Rick Stewart/Getty Images: 17. John Mottern/AFP/Getty Images: 23. M. David Leeds/Getty Images: 26. Jeff Carlick/MLB Photos/Getty Images: 29. Rich Pilling/MLB Photos/Getty Images: 31. Todd Warshaw/Getty Images: 33. Vincent Laforet/ Getty Images: 38. Mike Fiala/AFP/Getty Images: 40. Jed Jacobsohn/Getty Images: 47. K.C. Alfred/Union-Tribune/ Getty Images: 49. Courtesy of John Boggs: 51. Jim Esterbrooks, Courtesy of Jane Mitchell: 52. Courtesy of Jane Mitchell, Channel 4 San Diego: 53. John Reid III/MLB Photos/Getty Images: 61. Robert J. Galbraith/Getty Images: 64.

G|W|Y|N|N

CONTENTS

On July 29, former Padre Tony Gwynn will bring a little bit of San Diego sunshine with him to upstate New York.

"Mr. Padre" will join the Orioles' "Iron Man" Cal Ripken Jr. and the two will be inducted, having played the entireties of their lengthy careers with a single team.

"There's no question which hat we're going to wear, which uniform we're going to wear," Gwynn said. "Cal is an Oriole, and Tony is a Padre. I feel good about that, and I think Cal feels great about that."

A California native, Gwynn played his college ball at San Diego State University, where he was also a standout

game. For a hitter like me, I had to do a lot of what I did."

Gwynn was a favorite from start to finish and fans showed their love for him, voting him as a starter in 11 of 15 of his All-Star appearances. And Gwynn continues to give back to his hometown, as the coach for his alma mater's baseball program. He spent the day before his election at practice.

"We finish the practice with a 'Go Aztecs,'" Gwynn said. "But when we got into our circle, the players chanted 'Hall of Fame.' I came apart."

And after the election was official, Gwynn remained humble, happy to be validated and relieved that he didn't break Tom Seaver's 98.8 percent approval rating.

WELCOME TO THE HALL

By | Staci Wolfson

in basketball, setting the school record for assists (game, season and career). But shortly after his debut with the Padres in 1982, it became clear that it was Gwynn's swing that was special.

That season was the only time the right fielder would hit below .300 and from then on, the numbers began to add up. Despite never hitting more than 17 home runs in a season, Gwynn racked up 3,141 hits over the course of his 20-year career. In 9,288 at-bats, he struck out only 434 times.

His stats quickly translated into national recognition. Gwynn has been the recipient of five Gold Gloves, seven Silver Slugger Awards and eight National League batting titles. He was able to maintain his dominance, completing his illustrious career with a .338 batting average.

Still, Gwynn, whose No. 19 is retired by the Padres, wasn't sure where a hitter like him would fit in the Hall of Fame scheme. There was little question for the voters, however, who elected him with a 97.6 percent approval rating, the seventh highest of all Hall of Famers.

"It's an unbelievable feeling to know that people think that what you did was worthy," Gwynn told reporters shortly after being notified of his election. "The type of player that I was doesn't get a whole lot of credit in today's

"I'm really happy the way things worked out," Gwynn said. "I didn't want to set the record. I didn't want the percentage to be an issue. I'm so glad I don't have to deal with that one. I'm never going to be up there with the big boppers.

"But I'm proud as heck. All the years I played, I had this day in mind. Deep down, I've known. There's a place in this world for the Punch-and-Judy hitters because that's what I am."

The induction will mean as much to San Diego as it does to Gwynn. Although five former Padres have been inducted into the Hall of Fame, Gwynn is the only one to have spent his entire career in San Diego. Rollie Fingers, Willie McCovey, Gaylord Perry, Ozzie Smith and Dave Winfield all represent San Diego in the Hall, but Gwynn is the only one to go in as a Padre.

Gwynn said to players like himself and Ripken, the home team pride is the best part.

"In my case, fans love the fact that they don't look at me as being greedy," he said. "They look at me as being loyal. They look at me as being a team guy. I think it works to our benefit that we played on one club. The most beautiful thing about my career is when you look at the back of my baseball card, there's just one team. That's sweet to me." □

A LIFELONG BASEBALL FAN, STACI WOLFSON IS AN ASSISTANT EDITOR FOR PRESSBOX.

PADRES IN THE HALL OF FAME

PLAYERS

ROLLIE FINGERS, P
1968-1985 (1977-1980)
114-118, 2.90 ERA, 1,299 SO

WILLIE McCOVEY, 1B
1959-1980 (1974-1976)
.270, 2,211 hits, 521 HR, 353 2B, 1,555 RBI

GAYLORD PERRY, P
1962-1983 (1978-1979)
314-265, 3.11 ERA, 3,534 SO

OZZIE SMITH, SS
1978-1996 (1978-1981)
.262, 2,460 hits, 402 2B, 580 SB, 793 RBI

DAVE WINFIELD, OF
1973-1995 (1973-1980)
.283, 3,110 hits, 465 HR, 540 2B, 1,833 RBI

(Years with the Padres)

HIGHEST VOTE PERCENTAGE FOR HALL OF FAME INDUCTEES

	Name	Year Inducted	% of Votes
1.	TOM SEAVER	1992	98.84%
2.	NOLAN RYAN	1999	98.79%
3.	CAL RIPKEN JR.	2007	98.53%
4.	TY COBB	1936	98.23%
5.	GEORGE BRETT	1999	98.19%
6.	HANK AARON	1982	97.83%
7.	**TONY GWYNN**	**2007**	**97.61%**
8.	MIKE SCHMIDT	1995	96.52%
9.	JOHNNY BENCH	1989	96.42%
10.	STEVE CARLTON	1994	95.82%
11.	BABE RUTH	1936	95.13%
	HONUS WAGNER	1936	95.13%
13.	WILLIE MAYS	1979	94.68%
14.	CARL YASTRZEMSKI	1989	94.63%
15.	BOB FELLER	1962	93.75%
16.	REGGIE JACKSON	1993	93.62%
17.	TED WILLIAMS	1966	93.38%
18.	STAN MUSIAL	1969	93.24%
19.	ROBERTO CLEMENTE	1973	92.69%
20.	JIM PALMER	1990	92.57%

From National Baseball Hall of Fame and Museum, BaseballHallofFame.org

The first sighting sticks with you, even after all these years, like a piece of sturdy adhesive. Here he was, this plump, little college point guard with a stylish afro and an uncanny ability to snake through traffic and find the open man with a pretty pass.

Think of a chubbier version of Jason Kidd. That's what Tony Gwynn looked like and played like at San Diego State University in the late 1970s. So, no, you weren't surprised when the then-San Diego Clippers drafted him. What surprised you was when shortly thereafter, the San Diego Padres drafted him.

Who knew that the kid who was far more famous about himself. He would always have a wonderful knack for making you feel comfortable.

The moments spin past like some kind of baseball Rolodex.

Seeing him win his first of an extraordinary eight batting titles. Watching him act like a little kid at Disneyland when he made it to his initial World Series. Remembering his funny little jump for joy when he slid home with the winning run in the 1994 All-Star Game.

But maybe most of all, watching him come to bat in that climactic seventh inning in the deciding game of the 1984 National League Championship Series. You

A CAREER TO REMEMBER

By | Steve Bisheff

in college for dribbling a basketball to the hoop than stroking a baseball into the gap would one day become one of the greatest hitters in major league history? Even Gwynn himself looks back at those days and admits basketball was his favorite sport.

"If I'd been 6-foot-3, there's no doubt in my mind I would have gone into the NBA instead," he said.

The sport of baseball can only heave a long, thankful sigh he didn't.

Anthony Keith Gwynn, who grew up hitting socks with a makeshift bat in his Long Beach backyard, was more than just a Hall of Fame player. More than the finest pure hitter since Ted Williams. More than a living San Diego icon who played his entire big league career in one town and now coaches baseball back where it all started for him, at San Diego State.

Gwynn, who is about to take his rightful place in the hallowed halls of Cooperstown, also was the game's Dr. Feel Good. As quick with a smile as he was with a line drive. As gracious and modest as he was tough to pitch to with the bases loaded in the bottom of the ninth. No one ever had to worry about approaching Gwynn. He would always have a kind word or a funny joke to tell

would have had to live through all the long, hard years of Padres' futility to understand the emotion that had been building in Jack Murphy Stadium that bright fall afternoon. And here was Gwynn, the symbol of hope, the All-Star who could finally lead the team and city to redemption, standing in the batter's box with two runners on. Rick Sutcliffe, 17-1 coming into the game, winner of 14 straight including a 13-0 shutout in Game 1, was on the mound.

Sutcliffe fired his best pitch and Gwynn hit it as solidly as he seemingly always did. But the hard shot barreled its way directly at Ryne Sandberg, the future Hall of Fame second baseman and one of the finest defensive players of all time. It looked like a sure double play, a routine 4-6-3, but then a funny thing happened. Call it luck, or maybe fate. Call it whatever you want, but just as the ball got to Sandberg, it took a huge, crazy hop over his head for a double that drove in two runs to catapult the Padres to a 6-3 victory and their first World Series.

How appropriate. How perfect. The greatest player in franchise history getting the biggest hit. Padre fans still swear the noise that day at the ballpark was the loudest they've ever heard in San Diego.

– A Career To Remember –

If the flood of memories sometimes seems to run together, what is different with Gwynn is that it's the personal things you remember best. The many times he would wave you over and ask you to join him in the corner of the dugout, patiently chatting and answering every question for 40 minutes.

Especially that one session, in the summer of 1994. He was sitting quietly in the visiting dugout at Dodger Stadium. And for the first time I could recall, Gwynn turned somber. In a voice choked with emotion, he explained that his father Charles had died suddenly that past winter at 61, attempting to recover from severe flu symptoms in a hospital.

"He had a massive heart attack in a room with five doctors all around him," Gwynn said. "There was nothing they could do. Before he went, he told me there were two things he wanted me to do. He wanted me to win a fifth batting title. And he said he thought I was capable of hitting .400."

If anyone was capable of becoming the first to average .400 since Williams in 1941, it was Gwynn, the ultimate contact hitter who struck out only 434 times in 9,288 at-bats. The guy whose .338 lifetime average is the highest among players whose careers began after World War II.

And in that same year, inspired by his father's last wish, Gwynn made a grand run at it. In fact, from July 1, 1993 through June 30, 1994, he hit .399. "I was swinging the bat better than I ever did in my life," he said.

He was lighting up ESPN's nightly highlights and hitting a sweet .394 when baseball's strike shut down the game for the rest of the summer.

"That was definitely the best shot I ever had at it," Gwynn would say later. "We'll never know, of course, but I honestly think if we'd been able to finish the full season, I could have done it."

Baseball historians always want to argue about Gwynn's place in the stratosphere of great players. They're quick to acknowledge his 3,141 hits and his five 200-hit seasons. But they sneer at his lack of power and claim he doesn't belong with some of the all-time best because he wasn't a big-time run producer.

Gwynn, who always led the league in self-deprecation, would often question his own status. "Am I better than Hank Aaron? Stan Musial? Frank Robinson?" he would ask. "No way. The only thing I want people to say about me is that I played the game the way it should be played."

No one ever claimed otherwise. But while you had to admire Gwynn's modesty, you couldn't take away any of his magical numbers. "He was the best pure hitter of his generation," said Bruce Bochy, who was his longtime manager with the Padres.

He might have been even more than that. In one five-year stretch, from 1993-97, starting when he was 33, Gwynn averaged .371. Only five players in history ever had a better five-year run – Rogers Hornsby, Ty Cobb, Dick Sisler, Harry Heilmann and Al Simmons. And all of them began their streaks in their 20s.

Los Angeles Angels manager Mike Scioscia was a Dodgers catcher during the years when Gwynn was in his

DURING HIS ROOKIE SEASON IN 1982, TONY GWYNN APPEARED IN 54 GAMES AND BATTED .289.

TONY GWYNN CAREER STATISTICS

Regular Season

SEASON	G	AB	R	H	2B	3B	HR	RBI	BB	SO	SB	OBP	SLG	AVG
1982	54	190	33	55	12	2	1	17	14	16	8	.337	.389	.289
1983	86	304	34	94	12	2	1	37	23	21	7	.355	.372	.309
1984	158	606	88	213	21	10	5	71	59	23	33	.410	.444	.351
1985	154	622	90	197	29	5	6	46	45	33	14	.364	.408	.317
1986	160	642	107	211	33	7	14	59	52	35	37	.381	.467	.329
1987	157	589	119	218	36	13	7	54	82	35	56	.447	.511	.370
1988	133	521	64	163	22	5	7	70	51	40	26	.373	.415	.313
1989	158	604	82	203	27	7	4	62	56	30	40	.389	.424	.336
1990	141	573	79	177	29	10	4	72	44	23	17	.357	.415	.309
1991	134	530	69	168	27	11	4	62	34	19	8	.355	.432	.317
1992	128	520	77	165	27	3	6	41	46	16	3	.371	.415	.317
1993	122	489	70	175	41	3	7	59	36	19	14	.398	.497	.358
1994	110	419	79	165	35	1	12	64	48	19	5	.454	.568	.394
1995	135	535	82	197	33	1	9	90	35	15	17	.404	.484	.368
1996	116	451	67	159	27	2	3	50	39	17	11	.400	.441	.353
1997	149	592	97	220	49	2	17	119	43	28	12	.409	.547	.372
1998	127	461	65	148	35	0	16	69	35	18	3	.364	.501	.321
1999	111	411	59	139	27	0	10	62	29	14	7	.381	.477	.338
2000	36	127	17	41	12	0	1	17	9	4	0	.364	.441	.323
2001	71	102	5	33	9	1	1	17	10	9	1	.384	.461	.324
Totals:	2,440	9,288	1,383	3,141	543	85	135	1,138	790	434	319	.388	.459	.338

Postseason

Year	Round	Opp	W/L	G	AB	R	H	2B	3B	HR	RBI	BB	SO	SB	OBP	SLG	AVG
1984	NLCS	CHC	W	5	19	6	7	3	0	0	3	1	2	0	.381	.526	.368
1984	WS	DET	L	5	19	1	5	0	0	0	0	3	2	1	.364	.263	.263
1996	NLDS	STL	L	3	13	0	4	1	0	0	1	0	2	1	.308	.385	.308
1998	NLDS	HOU	W	4	15	1	3	2	0	0	2	0	2	0	.200	.333	.200
1998	NLCS	ATL	W	6	26	1	6	1	0	0	2	1	2	0	.259	.269	.231
1998	WS	NYY	L	4	16	2	8	0	0	1	3	1	0	0	.529	.688	.500
Totals:				27	108	11	33	7	0	1	11	6	10	2	.339	.398	.306

– A Career To Remember –

prime. He knows, better than most, how difficult it was to get the finest pure hitter of his generation out.

"He had the fewest holes of any hitter I've ever seen," Scioscia said. "He could inside-out a ball better than anyone who ever put a uniform on and that allowed him to wait on pitches longer than anyone else. On top of that, he was one of the most intelligent players I've ever been around. He knew how to work a count, when to drive a ball, when to go the other way. He had such great balance at the plate, it allowed him to have almost the perfect approach."

In the twilight of his career, Scioscia signed a contract with the Padres in 1993, then was injured just before the season started. But he had the opportunity to spend the entire year in San Diego observing Gwynn up close.

"The amount of work he would put in, the preparation involved was unbelievable," Scioscia said. "He was always working hard to maintain his skills and his swing. He adapted very well to any injuries he had. … He was just amazing.

"Early in his career, there was really nobody around him in the Padres' lineup, no other hitters you really feared. So you would go into the game intent on not letting him beat you. And he still did. Tony was just the best I ever saw."

- -

It was a sun-splashed, melancholy day in 2001 when Gwynn was supposed to make the formal announcement that he intended to retire at the end of the season. Before the scheduled press conference, Gwynn looked uncharacteristically ill at ease, standing at a podium next to his eight glittering silver bats, wearing jeans, a blue polo shirt and a matching baseball cap.

"I've never seen him so nervous," said his wife, Alicia. "He

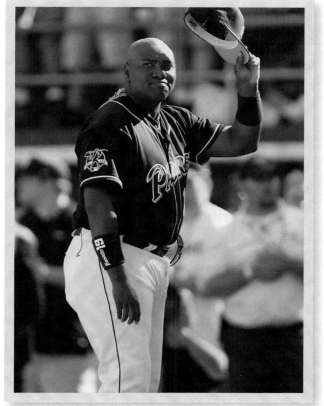

TONY GWYNN SALUTES THE CROWD DURING CEREMONIES PRIOR TO THE FINAL GAME OF HIS CAREER ON OCT. 7, 2001.

was pacing around the house all day. I just told him to go out there and be yourself."

And that's what Gwynn did. He was his usual, self-deprecating, likable self, saying he was not sure he would make it into the Hall of Fame with Cal Ripken on the first ballot, even though everyone knew he was a lock. He admitted it took him a while to come to his retirement decision and that it was "a sad day, but a happy one too."

Gwynn must have told me 100 times that his biggest thrill in baseball was running out on to the field every night. He truly loved to play the game. Like Ripken, it was a joy for him just to come to the ballpark each day.

"He and Ripken are remarkably parallel," said Larry Lucchino, the Padres' president at the time. "They were both the personification of their franchises."

Gwynn was more than just the face of the Padres – he was the face of San Diego. The once quiet but now sprawling town tucked between Los Angeles and the Mexican border has never had anyone, athlete or otherwise, who was a more popular figure than Tony Gwynn.

They admired him because he was so loyal to the city and the team. On numerous occasions, Gwynn could have filed for free agency and earned twice the salary he was paid by the Padres, but he wouldn't do it. He loved playing and living there too much. And the fans, in turn, loved him as much for his work ethic as his talent.

They called him "Captain Video" because he spent so much time studying tape. But he claimed he never would have been as good a hitter without it. Same with his fielding. He was below average defensively when he joined the Padres. By sheer hard work, by coming to the

– A Career To Remember –

TONY GWYNN
CAREER AWARDS

1995: Branch Rickey Award

1998: Lou Gehrig Memorial Award

1999: Roberto Clemente Award

GOLD GLOVES:

1986 (NL-OF)	1987 (NL-OF)	1989 (NL-OF)
1990 (NL-OF)	1991 (NL-OF)	

SILVER SLUGGERS:

1984 (NL-OF)	1986 (NL-OF)	1987 (NL-OF)	1989 (NL-OF)
1994 (NL-OF)	1995 (NL-OF)	1997 (NL-OF)	

* The Silver Slugger Awards are given each year to the best offensive player at each position in each league.

ALL-STAR GAMES:

Tony Gwynn was named to 15 All-Star teams:

1984	1985	1986	1987	1989
1990	1991	1992	1993	1994
1995	1996	1997	1998	1999

park early every day, he eventually won five Gold Gloves.

"People ask me about ballplayers and I've seen them all," said Jerry Coleman, the Padres' longtime broadcaster. "I've seen some greats, some wonderful home run hitters and strikeout pitchers. But the question I always want answered is, 'What kind of man was he?' Tony was the best."

As soon as the date was set, they knew. "We have to be there," the father said. "No question," agreed the son.

Tony Gwynn's last major league game was one of those events that didn't even merit a discussion. Their presence was taken for granted. The father is a sportswriter who worked in San Diego when his two sons were growing up. Now both boys have graduated from college and are busy settling into productive adult lives.

Happily though, a strong baseball connection remains, especially between the father and the youngest son.

The connection's name is Tony Gwynn.

The father covered him and the son loyally followed his favorite player through Gwynn's glory years in San Diego. Many happy hours were spent discussing the great hitter both loved to watch. As the nostalgic summer of 2001 slowly slipped away, it seemed to startle them that 20 years had passed.

Now here they were, driving from Los Angeles to San Diego together on a bittersweet October Sunday to watch Tony's last game.

"Is this a sad day for you?" the father asked.

"Yeah," the son admitted.

If life was fair, Gwynn, appearing only as a pinch hitter in the bottom of the ninth that day, would have stroked a single through what he called the 5.5 hole, between third and short. Ted Williams homered in his last at-bat, didn't he? Why shouldn't Gwynn single in his? Alas, it wasn't to be. Gwynn hit the ball hard, but right at shortstop Jose Uribe, who threw him out.

The father grimaced. The son said "Shoot!" The crowd groaned. But the warm, emotional 75-minute post-game tribute helped soothe any hard feelings.

With Bob Costas in town to emcee, they relived the points of Gwynn's glorious career, even bringing in members of his first team, the 1982 Padres. The Garry Templetons, Terry Kennedys and Luis Salazars all trotted out to man their original positions. And Anthony Gwynn Jr., Tony's son, who was playing at San Diego State University at the time, also trotted out.

Phil Nevin, Ryan Klesko and members of the Padres that year presented Gwynn with a shiny, new Harley Davidson motorcycle. "Just the thing a guy getting ready to have knee surgery should have," Gwynn cracked later.

Costas announced that the new Padres' downtown ballpark, the one that was due to open three years later, would be located at 19 Tony Gwynn Drive. And all the old San Diego team members, from Dave Winfield to Steve Garvey, were there to help him celebrate. "It's been a wonderful trip," Gwynn said, fighting back the tears.

Then the model for loyalty, dignity and humility, the wonderful gentleman ballplayer, waved goodbye and slowly took one final lap around Qualcomm Stadium. "I didn't think I'd do that," Gwynn said. "But it was really nice. The fans were really friendly."

At that tear-jerking point, my son proceeded to nudge me with an elbow and pointed out one 20-something standing proudly in the crowd. The man held up a poster that read:

"My Dad had Musial. I have Gwynn."

My son and I looked at each other and smiled. We didn't have to say the obvious. For us, it was different. For us, the hero was one and the same.

For us, we'll both always have Tony Gwynn. ☐

STEVE BISHEFF SPENT 42 YEARS AS A SPORTSWRITER AND COLUMNIST IN SOUTHERN CALIFORNIA AND IS THE AUTHOR OF FOUR BOOKS, THE LATEST BEING "FIGHT ON! THE COLORFUL STORY OF USC FOOTBALL" (CUMBERLAND HOUSE).

Long before there was a Tony Gwynn Stadium at San Diego State University, there was Tony Gwynn, the point guard.

Seriously.

While Gwynn honed his baseball skills playing for Jim Dietz at SDSU, he originally came to the school on a basketball scholarship.

Gwynn may not look like a point guard now, but as he prepares to enter baseball's Hall of Fame, there are still a few reminders of his long-ago hoops career.

There's not a lot of tradition and history associated with

You know, hey, for the time, I did what point guards did. Tried to penetrate all the time, dish."

Gwynn laughs his hearty belly laugh and expresses surprise when he thinks about his assists records – 18 in a game against UNLV on Feb. 5, 1980; 221 during the 1979-80 season; and 590 for his career.

"But to me that's how the game has evolved, though," he said. "Back in my days, point guards weren't scorers. Point guards were distributors. And now in today's game, a lot of your point guards are the best scorers too. Assists were like my points. That's how you made your

IT ALL STARTED ON THE HARDWOOD

By | B.J. Wilson

San Diego State basketball, at least not compared with that school up the freeway, UCLA, or other national powers. The Aztecs have never won an NCAA tournament game in five tries and it was just 10 years ago that they finally joined the rest of the modern hoops world in getting a nice campus arena.

But Gwynn's name is and always will be associated with the program at a school that's otherwise known for its reputation for partying.

Gwynn is one of only 17 Aztecs picked in the NBA Draft, chosen by the then-San Diego Clippers on the same day he was drafted by the San Diego Padres.

That, and his records for assists in a game, season and career still stand all these years later.

"I was a pretty good little point guard, but I didn't score," said Gwynn, who's now the baseball coach at his alma mater. "These guys kill me about how I played four years here and I didn't score 1,000 points. I got like 950 or something. I was a typical point guard – wasn't much of a scorer, but I'd run the offense, play pretty good defense, steal the ball, dish the ball.

statement on how good a player you were.

"I'm shocked. My last game was '81, so those records have been on the books for 26 years. Game, season and career. I really thought there were guys who would come in and break it. Even in today's game standards, they're just middle of the road. But 18 in a game was pretty good."

Tim Vezie, the basketball coach who recruited Gwynn to SDSU, really isn't surprised that those records haven't been broken.

"It shows you what kind of player Tony was," said Vezie, who coached Gwynn for two seasons. "He was the lead guy, a coach on the floor. He was always looking to get his teammates the ball. He could have been a much higher scorer if he wanted to. He became a much better shooter, but he was an assists man, looking to help his teammates score."

There was something else that stood out, just like it did during Gwynn's phenomenal run as the Padres' batting star.

"He was left-handed," Vezie said. "To me that was a real

– It All Started On The Hardwood –

plus to be able to find the open man. It caused problems for the defense."

After enrolling at SDSU, Vezie told Gwynn to focus on basketball his first two seasons. Gwynn, however, really wanted to play both basketball and baseball.

"Actually, I wanted him to focus on hoops the whole time he was there," Vezie said. "He wanted to play [baseball]; I just didn't want him to play."

That lasted only one season.

"His coach was Jim Dietz," Vezie said. "Jim asked me about Tony playing baseball and Tony asked me the same thing. I thought, 'Shoot, if it's best for him, that's what we should do.' I wouldn't let him play the first year. I told him, 'Tony, you're on a full basketball scholarship, I want you to develop your game.' The rest is history. The first year he went out there and hit some phenomenal average. That showed that he was also a good baseball player."

After talking to Dietz, Vezie realized that playing baseball wouldn't affect Gwynn's hoops game at all. "He still progressed as a basketball player all through his career," Vezie said.

Gwynn said he played a little more basketball than everyone expected he would as a freshman.

"That first year, Coach Vezie really wanted me to focus on basketball stuff and since I was on a basketball scholarship there was nothing I could say," Gwynn said. "I came here because I wanted to play both baseball and basketball and was told I was going to be given the chance. After the first year of not playing, I told Coach Vezie I was going to play baseball, no matter. He was fine with it."

Although he couldn't play baseball as a freshman, Gwynn still went to the games. He watched from Ragger's Rail, an area within earshot of the visiting team's bullpen.

"That's when I really missed it," Gwynn said. "At the time, I thought basketball was going to be my best option. That year I redshirted, I sat out on Ragger's Rail, I really missed the game and I really wanted to play again. So it worked out, but that first year I was bumming because I really wanted to be out there but Coach Vezie didn't want me to be out there."

While playing both sports, Gwynn would finish the hoops season before turning his full attention to baseball, although he sometimes would sneak down to the yard to practice.

"We usually finished March 1," he said. "My senior year, I played baseball the very next day."

Gwynn remembers playing a hoops game on a Saturday night and scoring 16 points with 16 assists.

"Then the very next day, I came down here and played baseball," he said. "I had been practicing before. I cheated and came down and practiced and went like 6-for-8 in a doubleheader and drove in a few runs and scored a few."

Vezie was fired after Gwynn's second season and replaced by Smokey Gaines. Gwynn and Gaines didn't always get along.

"I was really looking forward to playing baseball the last two years because Smokey and I didn't really see eye to eye on this stuff," Gwynn said. "In fact, my senior year I walked out of practice one day, thinking

TONY GWYNN STILL HOLDS THE SAN DIEGO STATE RECORDS FOR ASSISTS IN A GAME, SEASON AND CAREER.

– It All Started On The Hardwood –

'I don't need this, I'm going to go play baseball.'

"Coach Dietz made me go back and apologize. He said, 'You've been here for four years, you might as well go finish your career, then come down here and play baseball. We're going to be here.'

"I had to go back, apologize to Smokey. As it turned out, I had the best eight games of my career at the end. I just said, 'You know what, Coach is right, I've been here four years. I might as well go out with a bang.'"

SDSU fell just short of making it to the NIT that season. "So the next day I came down to baseball and started my baseball season," Gwynn said.

Dietz remembered that story as if it were yesterday. He said it was an important lesson that any young athlete needed to learn. It just happened that this was a future Hall of Famer.

"He came to me one year and said, 'I want to quit basketball,'" Dietz said. "I said, 'No, you can't do that.' He said, 'Well, I think I got a better shot at baseball.' I said, 'I would agree with that, but you started something, I want you to finish it.'

"He disagreed with me, but he stuck it out. There's a lesson to be learned. I see it all the time. Once you start something with a team, good, bad or indifferent, you've got to stick it out. That was the message I tried to get across. We butted heads. We still do. Everything I did was to try to help him."

Dietz could see how good Gwynn was in both sports.

"He really liked basketball," said Dietz, now retired and living in Oregon. "I think down inside today he still likes basketball. He was very good. He was an outstanding point guard. He really carried that Aztec team. Maybe

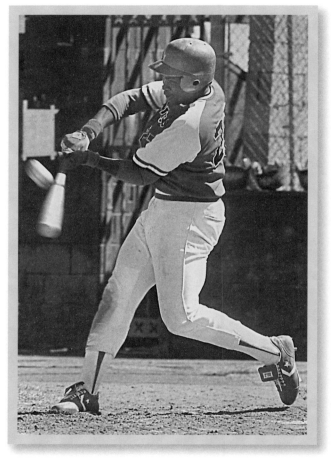

AFTER PLAYING JUST BASKETBALL HIS FRESHMAN YEAR, TONY GWYNN GOT THE CHANCE TO JOIN THE AZTECS BASEBALL TEAM.

not with points scored, but the role of point guard was not to score a lot of points, but be a leader.

"He could handle a ball, make decisions. He reminded me a lot of Steve Nash. Steve is not the biggest guy, not the fastest guy, but he is the smartest guy. That's the way Tony was. Great athletic instincts. I think he could have played in the NBA a little bit. Knowing Tony, it probably would have been a lot. At that stage of his life, he could do some unique things."

Then again, Dietz also saw how Gwynn could hit.

"He was the kind of kid who would lean toward the sport that was going on," Dietz said. "I would have to say if it was basketball season, that was his favorite. If it was baseball season, that was his favorite. He could have been a hell of a quarterback for the Aztecs too, just because he could make decisions."

Vezie also got the feeling that basketball was No. 1 with Gwynn, at least early on.

"Tony's a humble, quiet guy, modest. He just really wanted to play," Vezie said. "I really believe, and maybe I'm wrong on this, but I believe his first love was basketball. He really loved basketball. He loved baseball too, don't misunderstand me, but he really loved basketball. It was his first passion. If you ever watched him play, the desire he had, it was a natural sport for him. Baseball was too, but I think his real love at the time was basketball."

Of course, that's the problem. Not a lot of people got to watch him play hoops, since it was so long ago and before the advent of cable TV.

"He was so doggone good at it," Vezie said. "People

– It All Started On The Hardwood –

don't realize how good he was unless they saw him play. He would turn people upside down with his quickness and speed. His acceleration was unparalleled, as far as I was concerned. He was one of those guys who was a real leader by nature. He made everybody else better."

Gwynn was drafted by the Clippers in the 10th round in 1981. Vezie said the Clippers' general manager told him Gwynn would have gone higher, perhaps in the fourth round, but everyone knew he was going to end up playing baseball.

"He was good enough to be drafted," Vezie said. "He was the best point guard in the conference by far. He was a fabulous basketball player. He was one of the

"I THINK HE COULD HAVE PLAYED IN THE NBA A LITTLE BIT. KNOWING TONY, IT PROBABLY WOULD HAVE BEEN A LOT."

– Jim Dietz –

best point guards I've ever seen and the best point guard anyone at San Diego State has seen even to these days. That's why I recruited him to play basketball."

Although Gwynn and Gaines, who followed Vezie, didn't always get along, Gaines didn't limit Gwynn to just hoops.

Of course, Gwynn wouldn't have accepted that.

"I was playing baseball anyway," Gwynn said. "If he was going to take my scholarship, I was going to figure out another way to get it done. Smokey didn't and I played baseball and the rest is kind of history." □

B.J. WILSON COVERED THE SECOND HALF OF TONY GWYNN'S CAREER WITH THE PADRES.

TOP 58 PICKS IN THE 1981 MLB DRAFT		
1 Mike Moore (1982-1995)	21 John Cerutti (1985-1991)	41 Rick Rodriguez (1986-1990)
2 Joe Carter (1983-1998)	22 David Anderson (1983-1992)	42 Lanell Culver
3 Dick Schofield (1983-1996)	23 Dave Leeper (1984-1985)	43 Nelson Simmons (1984-1987)
4 Terry Blocker (1985-1989)	24 Al Lachowicz (1983)	44 Mike Fuentes (1983-1984)
5 Matt Williams (1983-1985)	25 Kevin Burrell	45 Chris Howard
6 Kevin McReynolds (1983-1994)	26 Frank Castro	46 C.L. Penigar
7 Daryl Boston (1984-1994)	27 Kevin Dukes	47 Scott Roberts
8 Bobby Meacham (1983-1988)	28 Darrin Jackson (1985-1999)	48 Sid Bream (1983-1994)
9 Ron Darling (1983-1995)	29 Jeff Carl	49 Tony Ferreira (1985)
10 Mark Grant (1984-1993)	30 Chuckie Canady	50 Lemmie Miller (1984)
11 Mike Sodders	31 Bill Pinkham	51 Craig Henderson
12 Jay Roberts	32 Bill Long (1985-1991)	52 John Elway
13 George Alpert	33 Mike Gallego (1985-1997)	53 Phil Bradley (1983-1990)
14 Jim Winn (1983-1988)	34 Mark Gubicza (1984-1997)	54 Mitch Cook
15 Tim Pyznarski (1986)	35 Mark Langston (1984-1999)	55 John Marzano (1987-1998)
16 Vance Lovelace 1988-1990)	36 Kelvin Torve (1988-1991)	56 Curt Wardle (1984-1985)
17 Ricky Barlow	37 Frank Viola (1982-1996)	57 Glenn Gallagher
18 Darren Dilks	38 John Christensen (1984-1988)	58 TONY GWYNN (1982-2001)
19 Steve Lyons (1985-1993)	39 Neal Heaton (1982-1993)	(YEARS IN MAJORS)
20 Johnny Abrego (1985)	40 Lee Tunnell (1982-1989)	

In a career that lasted 20 seasons and more than 2,400 games, Tony Gwynn provided baseball with its greatest hitter since Ted Williams. Seven Silver Slugger awards, 15 All-Star appearances and 3,141 hits ensured Gwynn would be an easy selection to the Hall of Fame, despite the fact that he never won an MVP award or a World Series title.

On Aug. 6, 1999, Gwynn entered baseball's prestigious 3,000-hit club by smacking a single to right-center field against Montreal Expos pitcher Dan Smith. Ty Cobb and Nap Lajoie are the only two players in baseball history to reach this plateau

third place in MVP voting that year. During the eight seasons in which he won a batting championship, Gwynn's average was .356.

Gwynn won three straight titles from 1987-'89 and a strike-shortened season in 1994 couldn't prevent him from winning his fifth. After winning three more batting titles from 1995-'98, Gwynn joined Cobb as the only players in major league history to win three consecutive titles on two separate occasions.

While Gwynn's first batting title helped his team to a National League pennant, other crowns did not lead to team success. In 1987, his Padres finished with the worst record in the NL, a disappointing 65-

THE EIGHT-TIME CHAMPION

By | Dean Jones Jr.

in fewer games than Gwynn, who took 2,284 games. (Cobb accomplished the feat in 2,135 games and Lajoie in 2,224 games.)

What sets Gwynn's hitting achievements apart from other players of his era are his remarkable eight batting titles and career .338 batting average. The batting titles tied Gwynn with Honus Wagner for the most in National League history. Gwynn ranks among the top 20 all time in batting average and his .338 career average is the highest since Williams retired in 1960 with a .344 average.

The eight batting crowns demonstrate Gwynn's knack for swinging the lumber in every situation imaginable, from his first at-bat – a sacrifice fly off Philadelphia Phillies' starter Mike Krukow on July 19, 1982 – to the next-to-last at-bat of his illustrious career – an RBI double off Colorado Rockies' reliever Gabe White on Oct. 6, 2001.

Each of the eight batting titles came under varying circumstances. The first, in 1984, helped Gwynn lead the Padres to the World Series. Despite losing to the Detroit Tigers in five games, Gwynn emerged as the future leader of the franchise, finishing in

97. Also, when the strike began in 1994, the Padres were at the bottom of the league, 47-70, even though Gwynn was flirting with becoming the first player to hit .400 since Williams in 1941.

The best way to show the significance of Gwynn's eight titles is by chronicling the details surrounding each of them.

1984: THE EMERGENCE OF "CAPTAIN VIDEO"

VCRs were once considered an expensive piece of modern technology without a place in society. Some people used them to tape television sitcoms that they could then watch over and over again, while others used them to watch amateur home videos.

Gwynn had a different idea, however, one that began to take shape in his rookie season in 1982 and would revolutionize the way professional baseball players approach hitting. Gwynn earned the nickname "Captain Video" from his teammates because he had his wife Alicia record his at-bats in order to correct his mistakes and continue to develop. The idea of using video technology as a hitting strategy was born

– The Eight-Time Champion –

and its father was on his way to his first batting title.

After two years as a part-time player, Gwynn was given the opportunity to be the Padres' starting right fielder. It was an opportunity that he seized and, with the exception of 1989 when he split time between center and right, did not let go for more than 16 seasons.

Gwynn stepped into the Padres' lineup that year and led San Diego to its first National League pennant. Teamed with Steve Garvey, Garry Templeton and Graig Nettles, Gwynn always seemed to come up with the big hit and he led the majors with 213.

No real competition challenged Gwynn in his quest for his first batting title. Lee Lacy and Chili Davis, hitters with career averages of .286 and .274 respectively, were his closest competitors. The final margin of victory in the first batting title was .351-.321, one of the largest margins of Gwynn's career. The triumph led Gwynn to a third-place finish in NL MVP voting, the best finish of his career.

Of Gwynn's 213 hits, 177 were singles, demonstrating his ability to put the ball in play while not necessarily hitting for power. He struck out only 23 times in 606 at-bats, an average of 26.3 times at the plate per strike-out. That statistic continued to exemplify Gwynn's plate discipline throughout his career. Since 1984, only one other player – Ozzie Smith (1993) – has averaged more at-bats between strikeouts in a single season, but Gwynn bettered that mark four other times in his career.

1984 NL BATTING LEADERS					
Name	Team	G	AB	H	AVG
Tony Gwynn	San Diego Padres	158	606	213	.351
Lee Lacy	Pittsburgh Pirates	138	474	152	.321
Chili Davis	San Francisco Giants	137	499	157	.315
Ryne Sandberg	Chicago Cubs	156	636	200	.314
Johnny Ray	Pittsburgh Pirates	155	555	173	.312

1987: ON-BASE MACHINE

In 1987, for the only time in his career, Gwynn reached base more than 300 times – 303 to be exact – and he did it in only 680 plate appearances. Gwynn reached base an amazing 45 percent of the time that season. Even more remarkably, Gwynn's on-base percentage was only good enough for second place

– The Eight-Time Champion –

behind the St. Louis Cardinals' Jack Clark. Clark and Gwynn had the top two on-base percentages for a single season in all of the 1980s.

After finishing fourth in batting average in 1985 (.317) and third in 1986 (.329), Gwynn regained his batting crown in 1987, hitting .370 and outdistancing the second-place finisher, Los Angeles Dodgers outfielder Pedro Guerrero. Gwynn hit 32 points higher than Guerrero and his final average was the highest to win the NL batting title since 1948 when Stan Musial hit .376.

Reaching base 303 times in a single season opened up other opportunities. In 1987, Gwynn set a career high with 56 stolen bases. Only one other time in his career did he steal more than 40 bases and only three other times more than 30. Gwynn finished second in stolen bases that year, but was no match for the leader, Vince Coleman, who stole 109 bases, his third straight season with more than 100.

During the 1987 campaign, Gwynn broke five team records, including two that he had set in 1984 – highest average and most hits in a season. Gwynn finished 1987 with 218 hits, which bested Guerrero's second-place tally of 184 by an astonishing 34 hits. His 34-hit margin was the largest in the NL since Musial had 40 hits more than Tommy Holmes did in 1948.

Gwynn also set the club record for runs scored in a single season with 119. Steve Finley broke that record with 126 runs in 1996, but the other two records Gwynn set in 1987 still stand today – 13 triples and 26 intentional walks.

1987 NL BATTING LEADERS					
Name	Team	G	AB	H	AVG
Tony Gwynn	San Diego Padres	157	589	218	.370
Pedro Guerrero	Los Angeles Dodgers	152	545	184	.338
Tim Raines	Montreal Expos	139	530	175	.330
John Kruk	San Diego Padres	138	447	140	.313
Dion James	Atlanta Braves	134	494	154	.312

1988: LOW, BUT STILL HIGHEST

Winning his second straight batting title and third in his first five complete seasons didn't come easy for Gwynn. Injuries plagued him for much of the early part of the season and his average suffered.

On March 11, Gwynn underwent surgery on his left hand to alleviate tendon pain and give it unlimited movement. Then, after a fall in Pittsburgh on May 7, Gwynn landed on the 21-day disabled list.

Gwynn's average dropped to .237 on June 3, the lowest mark that late in the season for his entire career. Going into July, his average was still sub-.250. Using an 18-game hit streak in the beginning of the month, Gwynn hit .406 in July to earn NL Player of the Month honors and bring his season average back up.

Gwynn eventually raised his average over .300, finishing the season at .313, good enough for a slim victory over the Chicago Cubs' duo of Rafael Palmeiro (.307) and Andre Dawson (.303).

Gwynn's .313 average was the lowest in NL history for a batting champion. Only Elmer Flick (.308) in 1905, Snuffy Stirnweiss (.309) in 1945 and Carl Yastrzemski (.301) in 1968 had lower averages while winning a batting title in major league history.

Gwynn struck out 40 times that year, the most in a single season in his career and the 163 hits were the fewest that Gwynn had for a single season in the 1980s. In the '80s, Gwynn had four 200-hit seasons, as well as a 197-hit season.

1988 NL BATTING LEADERS					
Name	Team	G	AB	H	AVG
Tony Gwynn	San Diego Padres	133	521	163	.313
Rafael Palmeiro	Chicago Cubs	152	580	178	.307
Andre Dawson	Chicago Cubs	157	591	179	.303
Andres Galarraga	Montreal Expos	157	609	184	.302
Gerald Perry	Atlanta Braves	141	547	164	.300

1989: DOWN TO THE LAST WEEKEND

A competitive head-to-head battle was never a part of Gwynn's first three batting titles. In 1984 and 1987, Gwynn won the batting titles in dominating fashion. The battle for the 1988 crown demonstrated a closer statistical finish than the previous two routs – a six-point victory – but the outcome was decided relatively early due to Gwynn's scorching start to the second half, hitting .406 in July.

– The Eight-Time Champion –

But 1989 brought a different challenge for Gwynn to conquer. The right fielder was locked in a duel with San Francisco Giants first baseman Will Clark that lasted until the final weekend of the season. The two players met for the final three games when Gwynn's Padres hosted Clark's Giants at Jack Murphy Stadium.

Since the Padres had dropped two out of three to the Cincinnati Reds in the previous series, the Giants had clinched the NL West. Therefore, the pursuit of the batting title provided the only drama in sunny southern California.

Gwynn once again delivered in the clutch, fighting through Achilles tendon and wrist injuries to give the hometown fans something to cheer about as their otherwise disappointing last week of the season played out. Gwynn went 6-for-8 to beat Clark .336 to .333 and capture his third straight title. The three-point margin represented the smallest spread of Gwynn's eight titles.

1989 NL BATTING LEADERS					
Name	Team	G	AB	H	AVG
Tony Gwynn	San Diego Padres	158	604	203	.336
Will Clark	San Francisco Giants	159	588	196	.333
Lonnie Smith	Atlanta Braves	134	482	152	.315
Mark Grace	Chicago Cubs	142	510	160	.314
Pedro Guerrero	St. Louis Cardinals	162	570	177	.311

1994: QUEST FOR .400

From 1990 to 1993, Gwynn maintained a batting average above .300 in each of the four seasons, including .358 in 1993. Unfortunately for Gwynn, Colorado Rockies first baseman Andres Galarraga had a career year, finishing 12 points ahead at .370.

Injuries and disappointment categorized those four seasons for Gwynn. In 1990, he fractured his right index finger while trying to catch a fly ball in Atlanta Sept. 15 and, as a result, missed the final 19 games. Gwynn's 1991 season ended Sept. 18 when he had arthroscopic surgery on his left knee. Then for the third straight season, Gwynn's season ended early, this time due to a sprained medial collateral ligament in his left knee.

Gwynn's 1993 season featured highlights overshadowed by severe lowlights. On Aug. 4, he had a career-high six hits in a 12-inning victory over the San Francisco Giants.

Gwynn also had three five-hit games and after leading the majors with a .448 batting average in August en route to NL Player of the Month honors, Gwynn appeared headed for his fifth batting title. But that mission was delayed another year when Gwynn underwent another arthroscopic surgery in his left knee, cutting his season short. To make matters worse, the Padres finished 61-101.

Gwynn needed a big rebound in 1994 and as usual, he again stepped up. Despite threats of a lockout or strike, Gwynn did what he could do best – hit the ball.

Throughout the 1994 season, Gwynn had fans and media clamoring for him to become the first .400 hitter since Williams. However, the season ended Aug. 12 when the Major League Baseball Players Association announced a strike. At the time, Gwynn was hitting .475 for the month and stood just .006 points away from .400 with only 45 games to play.

Still, Gwynn had rebounded from four straight years of season-ending injuries to capture his fifth batting title. And he did it easily, defeating second-place finisher Jeff Bagwell .394 to .368. Gwynn reached base 215 times out of 475 plate appearances in the shortened season, good enough for a .454 on-base percentage, the best of his career.

Gwynn's push for .400, and the season, ended prematurely. No one will ever know if Gwynn would have become the first player in more than 50 years to hit .400, but one thing was certain – he had recovered from the injuries of the past seasons to begin another impressive string of batting titles.

1994 NL BATTING LEADERS					
Name	Team	G	AB	H	AVG
Tony Gwynn	San Diego Padres	110	419	165	.394
Jeff Bagwell	Houston Astros	110	400	147	.368
Mike Kingery	Colorado Rockies	105	301	105	.349
Moises Alou	Montreal Expos	107	422	143	.339
Hal Morris	Cincinnati Reds	112	436	146	.335

1995: YOU CAN'T STRIKE HIM OUT

In 535 at-bats in 1995, Gwynn struck out only 15 times, giving him an average of 35.7 at-bats per strikeout. Gregg Jefferies of the Philadelphia Phillies finished second in

– The Eight-Time Champion –

that category and he struck out once every 18.5 at-bats, almost twice as frequently as Gwynn. The third-place finisher, Chicago Cubs first baseman Mark Grace, struck out three times as frequently as Gwynn.

Gwynn tied for the NL lead in hits with Colorado Rockies outfielder Dante Bichette. Both outfielders had 197 and the total represented Gwynn's highest hit count since he had 203, but he registered 69 fewer at-bats than in 1989.

One of Gwynn's hits was also the first of only three grand slams the right fielder had in his career. The bases-loaded shot came on Aug. 22 in the top of the fifth inning against Philadelphia Phillies starter Tommy Greene after 6,991 career at-bats.

Gwynn's .368 average bettered the second-place finisher, Los Angeles Dodgers catcher Mike Piazza (.346), by 22 points. Once again, Gwynn built his average up with singles, a league-leading 154 of them.

As was often the case, Gwynn out-hit a leading power hitter. In 1987, Guerrero slugged 27 home runs, but fell short of Gwynn's effective singles-hitting approach. Palmeiro, Dawson and Galarraga finished just behind Gwynn in 1988. Palmeiro has 569 career home runs, Dawson smashed 438 over 21 seasons and Galarraga finished with 399 in his career. In strike-shortened 1994, Jeff Bagwell hit 39 home runs in 110 games, while Gwynn finished with 12. This time, Piazza belted 32 home runs to Gwynn's nine.

requirement for minimum number of plate appearances has not been satisfied.

Rule 10.22(a) of the official rule book of Major League Baseball states:

Notwithstanding the foregoing requirement of minimum appearances at the plate, any player with fewer than the required number of plate appearances whose average would be the highest, if he were charged with the required number of plate appearances shall be awarded the batting, slugging or on-base percentage championship, as the case may be.

In 1996, Gwynn only played in 116 games due to an injured right Achilles tendon. He only had 498 official plate appearances – four short of the required 502 to qualify for a batting title.

However, thanks to Rule 10.22(a), Gwynn earned his third straight batting title. The rule permitted the four hitless at-bats necessary for Gwynn to get to the required 502 appearances to be added to his total. With the hypothetical at-bats added to his total, Gwynn's average would have dropped to .349. Since second-place finisher Ellis Burks had a .344 average, Gwynn remained the leader and therefore became batting champion once again. However, the final tally is etched in the record books at .353, the average accumulated in 498 plate appearances.

1995 NL BATTING LEADERS					
Name	Team	G	AB	H	AVG
Tony Gwynn	San Diego Padres	135	535	197	.368
Mike Piazza	Los Angeles Dodgers	112	434	150	.346
Dante Bichette	Colorado Rockies	139	579	197	.340
Derek Bell	Houston Astros	112	452	151	.334
Mark Grace	Chicago Cubs	143	552	180	.326

1996 NL BATTING LEADERS					
Name	Team	G	AB	H	AVG
Tony Gwynn	San Diego Padres	116	451	159	.353
Ellis Burks	Colorado Rockies	156	613	211	.344
Mike Piazza	Los Angeles Dodgers	148	547	184	.336
Lance Johnson	New York Mets	160	682	227	.333
Mark Grace	Chicago Cubs	142	547	181	.331

1996: RULE 10.22(A)

Although Rule 10.22(a) became part of MLB's code of rules in 1967, the passage served as little more than a precaution until 1996. The purpose of the clause is to give a player the opportunity to be crowned champion in an offensive category if his lead is large enough, but the

1997: SAVING THE BEST FOR LAST

Statistically, the last hitting hurrah of Gwynn's memorable career easily eclipsed the other seven titles. In 1997, Gwynn achieved career highs in home runs and RBIs. The 17 home runs surpassed his previous mark of 14, set in 1986, while the 119 RBIs destroyed his 1995 total of 90. Gwynn's third highest RBI total

– The Eight-Time Champion –

was 72 in 1990.

Gwynn's superstar season resulted in his name at the top of several NL leader boards at the conclusion of the 1997 season. In addition to his fourth straight batting title, Gwynn led the NL in hits with a career-high 220, and multi-hit games. For the ninth time in his career, Gwynn was the toughest player to strike out, averaging 21.1 at-bats per strikeout. And in a sign of his selfless nature even in the midst of a career season, Gwynn tied for the league lead with 12 sacrifice flies.

Meanwhile, his .372 batting average represented the second-highest total of his career, surpassed only by his .394 average in 1994. Gwynn needed every point to hold off Colorado Rockies right fielder Larry Walker and Piazza. Walker finished the season with a .366 average, while Piazza came in third at .363. Padres teammate Wally Joyner finished fifth with a .327 average.

Unfortunately for Gwynn, his offensive outbreak didn't help the Padres find success and the team finished the season 76-86 in fourth place in the NL West.

1997 NL BATTING LEADERS

Name	Team	G	AB	H	AVG
Tony Gwynn	San Diego Padres	149	592	220	.372
Larry Walker	Colorado Rockies	153	568	208	.366
Mike Piazza	Los Angeles Dodgers	152	556	201	.362
Kenny Lofton	Atlanta Braves	122	493	164	.333
Wally Joyner	San Diego Padres	135	455	149	.327

TY COBB, HONUS WAGNER AND TONY GWYNN

For 20 seasons, Tony Gwynn gave baseball aficionados a glimpse of what it was like to play baseball at the beginning of the 20th century. Gwynn excelled by hitting the ball everywhere between the lines and not aiming for the fences. Throughout his career, he consistently hit above .300, while rarely connecting on a long ball.

Wagner, the legendary Pittsburgh Pirates great, had a similar approach during his playing days from 1897-1917. While Wagner's career-high 10 home runs in a season was a lot for his era, he focused more on getting on base. The Flying Dutchman finished in the top 10 in the NL in hits 13 times, while Gwynn

TONY GWYNN FINISHED IN THE TOP 10 IN THE NL IN BATTING AVERAGE 15 TIMES DURING HIS CAREER:

1984: Ranked FIRST in the NL with .351 average

1985: Ranked FOURTH in the NL with .317 average

1986: Ranked THIRD in the NL with .329 average

1987: Ranked FIRST in the NL with .370 average

1988: Ranked FIRST in the NL with .313 average

1989: Ranked FIRST in the NL with .336 average

1990: Ranked EIGHTH in the NL with .309 average

1991: Ranked THIRD in the NL with .317 average

1992: Ranked FIFTH in the NL with .317 average

1993: Ranked SECOND in the NL with .358 average

1994: Ranked FIRST in the NL with .394 average

1995: Ranked FIRST in the NL with .368 average

1996: Ranked FIRST in the NL with .353 average

1997: Ranked FIRST in the NL with .372 average

1998: Ranked NINTH in the NL with .321 average

did the same thing 12 times. As the all-time leader for batting titles with 12, Detroit Tigers' outfielder Cobb also possessed similar statistics to Gwynn. Cobb led the American League in singles for six seasons, while Gwynn led the NL on seven different occasions.

Gwynn's batting titles put him in a class of his own; he is the only player in major league history to win four batting championships in two separate decades. Gwynn's four straight titles from 1994-'97 ties him for the third longest streak of all time with Wade Boggs and Rod Carew. Only Cobb and Rogers Hornsby have longer successive stretches.

Gwynn will be remembered as the greatest hitter of his generation and one of the finest in the history of the game. From his ability to hit any pitcher he faced, righty or lefty, to his revolutionary approach of analyzing video to improve his hitting, Gwynn humbly strived to be the best at what he did. Eight batting titles and a career .338 batting average guarantee his proper place in baseball's history books, right up there with the hitting greats of the early 20th century. ☐

DEAN JONES JR. CURRENTLY COVERS BASEBALL FOR SEVERAL WEB SITES AND IS A FREQUENT CONTRIBUTOR TO PRESSBOX.

Tony Gwynn felt like he knew Ted Williams well before he ever met the Hall of Fame slugger. After Gwynn arrived at San Diego State in the late 1970s, he certainly had heard of the Splendid Splinter, but he got a detailed education about San Diego's favorite son from baseball fans there, particularly since Gwynn wore No. 19 – the number Williams had worn when he was a scholastic baseball star at Herbert Hoover High School.

Little did Gwynn know there would be far more of a connection to Williams than a uniform number – a connection to the game they both loved and played with passion and excellence.

"I feel very fortunate to be one of those guys who knew him pretty well," Gwynn said. "I feel fortunate

runs over his career and drove in 100 runs just once, with 119 RBIs in 1997. Williams drove in more than 100 runs nine times over his playing tenure.

Oddly enough, it was those differing styles that kicked off the rich relationship between the two men.

The 1992 All-Star Game took place in San Diego and Williams was in attendance. Gwynn was already an established superstar of his time, having won four National League batting titles, and playing in his eighth All-Star Game over the first 11 years of his career. Gwynn made a point of trying to meet Williams, who made the experience seem larger than life, as was his style, when he took Gwynn's bat in his hand to make a point.

"He had his entourage, his security guards, his son and was on the third base line," Gwynn said. "I just walked

THE TED WILLIAMS EFFECT

By | Thom Loverro

to say he was a friend."

That in itself may be as great an accomplishment as the 3,141 hits Gwynn amassed over his 20-year career or his remarkable .338 career batting average. Williams could sometimes be as hard as the bats he used to hit 521 career home runs. He had high standards, and didn't suffer fools, but he loved Gwynn and the devotion the San Diego Padre outfielder had for hitting.

"Gwynn is like nobody of my era," Williams told the *San Diego Union-Tribune* in 2002. "Guys back then didn't get 3,000 hits. I didn't get 3,000 hits."

That's high praise from one of the greatest hitters ever to play the game.

"Ted Williams had a huge impact on my career," Gwynn said. "I didn't really know him all that long, but after I met him, I was a much better hitter. And I'd like to think we had a connection and there was some affection there."

As great a hitter as both of them were, they were obviously different types of hitters. Williams was far more of a power hitter than Gwynn, who hit 135 home

over and introduced myself. 'Hello, Mr. Williams. I am Tony Gwynn. I've heard a lot about you and read a lot about you.' He knew a little bit about me. He shook my hand and we started talking about hitting.

"I happened to have my bat in my hand, and he said, 'Is that what you swing?' I said, 'Yes sir.' I handed it to him, and I think he was shocked at how small it was, because after he picked it up, he started picking his teeth with it.

"He said, 'Do you swing this little thing?' I said, 'Yes, sir.' He said, 'Well, evidently, you are swinging well because you're hitting the ball all over the place.' It was one of those conversations where you introduce yourself just to let him know you are alive and then you go about your business. But the fact that he took my bat and picked his teeth with it really stuck with me. You are talking about one of the greatest hitters to ever play taking your bat and picking his teeth with it. I took it like he was telling me that maybe I should use a little bigger bat."

Gwynn made a slight change the following season, going to a longer but slightly lighter bat. But the conversation stuck with him, as did one he had when he was inducted into

– The Ted Williams Effect –

the Ted Williams Hitters Hall of Fame in Hernando, Fla. in 1994. Bob Costas was there conducting interviews with Williams and others in attendance. They had finished an interview with President George H.W. Bush when Costas asked Williams, "Who do you want to talk to now?"

Williams said, "Let's talk to that Tony Gwynn guy."

It is a legendary interview that has been seen a number of times and one that had a major impact on Gwynn.

"We get into this conversation, and I am trying to explain to him that the thing I do best is hitting the ball the other way," Gwynn said. "He is scolding me on it, telling me that history is made on hitting the ball inside. We go back and forth and I say, 'Mr. Williams, I don't have to hit that ball out of the ballpark. When they do come in and I handle it, I am letting the pitcher know that I can handle it.' He just laughed and laughed, and said, 'You have no idea.' He said again history is made on the ball inside, but he really didn't elaborate. He said, 'Pitchers are going to come in, and you have to show them you can handle the ball in.' I said, 'Mr. Williams, I do handle the ball in. I just don't hit it out of the ballpark.' Again, he laughed and the conversation sort of ended with that."

But it didn't end there for Gwynn. He kept rerunning the conversation over and over again.

"The whole flight home, I am sitting with my agent talking about what did he mean, history is made on hitting the ball inside." Gwynn said. "I don't get it. This was going into the 1995 season. So before spring training, I am working on that every day, trying to figure out what he is talking about. So from January 1995 to early in 1997, I am trying to figure out what he is talking about.

"Finally, it dawns on me what he meant. What he meant was if you hit the ball that's in out of the ballpark, they won't pitch you inside anymore. It took me until 1997 in the first half, after I hit 10 or 12 home runs, to

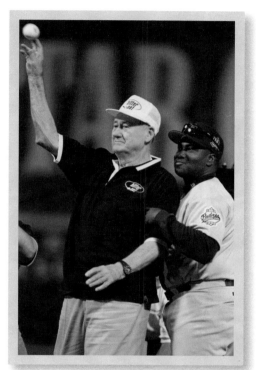

TONY GWYNN SUPPORTS TED WILLIAMS AS HE THROWS OUT THE CEREMONIAL FIRST PITCH BEFORE THE 1999 ALL-STAR GAME AT FENWAY PARK.

figure out what he was talking about.

"From the first conversation we had to that point in 1997, it took me that long to figure out that little bat and him picking his teeth, it was like a puzzle. You put the pieces of the puzzle together, to take a longer bat and be a little more aggressive on the ball inside. Most of the time in my career I had taken that ball inside and gone the other way. But when I started driving the ball – not necessarily hitting it out of the park, but driving the ball – pitchers started pitching to me the way I wanted to be pitched to. It took me that long to figure it out. When I did figure it out, 1997, I think was my best year – double figures in home runs and the only time in my career I drove in 100 runs."

Several years later, when Gwynn was being honored at a banquet in San Diego, Williams was there. Gwynn sought him out to thank him for the advice and to say how much of a better hitter he felt he was as a result of their conversation. Williams winked at him in approval.

Williams asked for Gwynn to be on the mound with him when he threw out the ceremonial first pitch at the All-Star Game in Boston in 1999. Gwynn braced Williams to make the throw to Carlton Fisk and then was there with Mark McGwire, Cal Ripken and others who surrounded Williams.

"It was nice to see him have a good time there and the players had a great time," Gwynn said.

Three years later, Williams died. Gwynn felt the loss and his time with Williams has only grown more special over the years. "He was one of the icons of the game and just having the opportunity to talk to him was enough for me," Gwynn said. "He made me a better player." □

THOM LOVERRO IS A COLUMNIST FOR THE WASHINGTON TIMES AND HAS PUBLISHED SEVERAL BOOKS, INCLUDING "HOME OF THE GAME: THE STORY OF CAMDEN YARDS".

They tell the story of when Bret Saberhagen first showed up in the National League with his true (old gun) 95-mph fastball and the former Kansas City Royals two-time Cy Young Award winner was at his nastiest. Tony Gwynn was apprised of his ability and the left-handed batter strode toward the plate saying, "Let's see."

Saberhagen unloaded a series of fastballs that Gwynn lined over the third base dugout, one after another. Finally, the pitcher said heck with this and he threw his excellent changeup plateward. Bang, Gwynn lined it up the middle for a single. Saberhagen backed off the mound, peered over at Gwynn on first base and asked, "How'd you do that?"

everything else going on on a ballfield, the real key to Gwynn's success was the swing.

"In some ways, Tony relates it to golf," Rettenmund said. "You work on it and work on it until you get it as good as you can and then you trust it. He's always telling the young players, 'Trust the swing.'"

Before joining the Padres in the '90s, Rettenmund led the Baltimore Orioles in hitting in back-to-back years in the early '70s when they were great. He also worked in the California, Texas and Oakland organizations as both a roving minor league instructor and big league batting coach before going to work for Atlanta, Detroit and Toronto.

"When I went to Atlanta, the Braves had it in their mind to have the catcher tell Tony what pitch was coming,"

TRUST THE SWING

By | Phil Jackman

Back in the dugout, Gwynn sat down beside San Diego Padres hitting coach Merv Rettenmund and said, "Watch, he's going to start me out with that changeup next time up." A couple of innings later, it was Saberhagen against Gwynn again.

Whoosh, there it went, a mid-90s heater. Gwynn was ready for it and smacked another single into center field. Again, the pitcher backed off the mound and inquired, "How'd you do that?" Gwynn smiled.

Later, Rettenmund asked the same question and got the same reply he always seemed to get from Gwynn: "I just saw the ball really good."

That simple, huh? Eyesight?

"Hardly," said Rettenmund, who had the pleasure of working with the short, squat outfielder for more than nine seasons as Gwynn made his way toward baseball's Hall of Fame. "More so than anyone else I've ever seen, Tony has the incredible ability to focus and concentrate for a split second and pick up what the pitcher is throwing. He sees the guy's fingers on the release. He's amazing. He sees what a guy's doing that quickly and says, 'OK, I got it.'"

In addition to studying pitchers, catchers, hitters and

Rettenmund said. "Tony hated that. All he wanted to do is see the ball and hit it on the barrel."

This simple approach is not unlike what Hank Aaron once said when it was apparent he had pretty well mastered the art of hitting on the big league level: "I see something white and hit it with a stick."

Then there was Hall of Famer Yogi Berra's famous line uttered when he was at bat one day and the catcher informed him that the trademark of his bat was in the wrong location and that he might shatter the wood: "I'm up here to hit, not read."

"I think Tony could always hit, probably going back to the day he first picked up a bat," Rettenmund said. "And I know his approach to hitting has always been the same. Half, if not more of what I've learned over the last 25 years [as a batting coach] comes from just watching him and talking to him. He's amazing (a commonly-used word when discussing Gwynn), and the thing is it isn't just hitting; he worked on every part of his game all the time.

"I don't care what kind of game he had the day before, he was always one of the first players at the park the next

– Trust The Swing –

day and with a big smile on his face. In that respect, a guy I think I'd liken him to and a guy I played with is Brooks Robinson. I don't know Cal Ripken that well, but from what I've heard, if Cal is baseball in Baltimore, Tony's the same thing in San Diego, no doubt."

Rettenmund got started "by accident" coaching hitters, just about the time Gwynn was graduating from San Diego State, where he was a dynamite baseball player after being recruited out of Long Beach as a highly-regarded basketball point guard.

"I started with the Angels and didn't know a darn thing," Rettenmund said. "I was the dumbest hitting coach in the major leagues and it probably would have stayed that way if I hadn't got to Oakland as a roving minor league instructor.

"All that mechanical talk is bull. Guys do it to sound smart. I was somewhere in the minors when I ran into a psychologist named Harvey Dorfman and he changed my whole perspective on the job. The fact is, if you can get the batter ready to swing, you've done your job. You've got to be ready. Your mind has to think preparation and you've got to commit."

By commit, Rettenmund means a player has to be ready to swing. "You commit even before you look at the action of the pitcher," he said. "If you don't, you get behind and you never catch up, not with the way guys are throwing these days."

Any doubts the coach had were quickly dispelled when he joined and became a teammate, coach, friend and confidant of Tony Gwynn. "I was in Oakland and in one of those typical clubhouse meetings, we were going over the hitters in the American League and maybe I went a little overboard on a few of them," Rettenmund said. "[Then-Oakland manager] Doug Rader says to me, 'Wait until you see the guy with the little hands and the little bat in San Diego.'"

It wasn't too much longer before it was time to check out the man with the wee hands and wee bat down by the

"TO TONY, IT'S ALL IN THE SWING. WORK ON IT CONSTANTLY AND WHEN YOU GET IT DOWN, TRUST THE SWING."

– Merv Rettenmund –

Mexican border. "To Tony, it's all in the swing," he said. "Work on it constantly and when you get it down, trust the swing."

That's been the Gwynn credo since even before he was drafted in the third round out of college in 1981. The only problem he had initially was adjusting from the aluminum bats used in college to the wooden bats used later on. Gwynn favored a 33-inch bat weighing 30.5 ounces and the only place he could find them was in a sporting goods store selling old wooden Little League bats in Eugene, Ore.

Somehow, those "toys" held up as he was making his way to The Show the next year, when he hit .289 in 54 games, the only year in which he batted under .309. He was on his way to a career mark of .338, the highest average ever for a batter starting his career after World War II.

"I go back over his numbers and I'm surprised they're not better," Rettenmund said. "All the [nine] years I was with him, I can't remember him hitting anything but .360. Wait a minute, there was the year he hit .394 or something."

Batting titles in '84, '87, '88, '89, '94, '95, '96 and '98 put Gwynn up there with Honus Wagner as the all-time leader in the National League despite the fact, said Rettenmund, he gave a couple away "because of a bad leg that always wore down late in the season."

"I remember one year he had about a 30-point lead on Terry Pendleton with less than a month to go and his knee was so bad he couldn't run at all. But Tony never sat down, ever. Pendleton beat him out."

Despite his concentration and focus when he was drawing a bead on a pitcher, Rettenmund said, "There are two pitchers who always gave Tony trouble, only two – Pedro Martinez and Randy Johnson.

"He says he could never pick up Pedro's changeup, which is the best in baseball, and Johnson throws three-quarter, which makes his release point difficult to pick

– Trust The Swing –

up. Unlike most hitters, Tony never worried about slumps, which were few and far between.

"He never stopped working on his swing, confident that if he kept that in line, come the end of the year he'd be there either winning the batting title or close. The swing, the swing, that's pretty much all he'd talk about.

"I remember one time he started complaining about not feeling comfortable at the plate. He didn't know what to do. Finally, he said, 'Next time up I'm going to drive the ball down the third base line.' Next time up, he smashes the ball down the line. He's out at first but comes back to the dugout and says, 'OK, I've got my confidence back.' And next time up he proved it by getting a single through what he called the '5.5 hole' between shortstop and third base."

As if a .338 lifetime average isn't good enough, it's scary to think what Gwynn might have batted if his weight wasn't a constant problem and his knee and legs had held up.

"After a while, Tony said he didn't worry about his weight, figuring it helped his balance," Rettenmund said. "But the bum knee was another story. It was his back knee, the one he pushed off with and toward the end of a season it always bothered him."

It wasn't something anyone would notice, because while constantly powdering away at a league-best average, he was picking up Gold Gloves, mainly as a right fielder. Once he moved over to center, he was the league's best there, too.

By 1994, his 13th season, and after several knee operations, Gwynn found himself hitting .390-plus and threatening to become the first player since Ted Williams in 1941 to hit .400. The streak goes back even further in the National League, to Bill Terry's .401 in 1930.

"Tony doesn't use it as an excuse," Rettenmund said, "but he says the reason he probably didn't make it is he never had hitting .400 as a goal until he was doing it. And he's so goal-oriented when it comes to hitting I think he would have made it had he set out to do it. Besides, he was just three hits short and with those legs…"

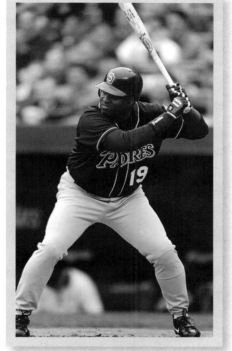

Besides the eight batting titles and five Gold Gloves, Gwynn was a terrific base stealer before leg problems pushed him more toward being a run producer instead of a run scorer. He stole 56 bases in 1987 (second in the NL) and finished with 319 total.

Beginning in 1993 and over the next five seasons, he averaged .369 while piling up most of his 543 doubles, 85 triples and 135 home runs on the way to 1,138 runs batted in. Not bad for a guy who almost refused to accept walks (790), rarely swung at the first pitch (he wanted a look), yet struck out just 434 times in 9,288 at-bats (once every 21 at-bats).

After smacking 3,141 hits and playing in 15 All-Star games before quitting at age 41 with a .324 batting average his last season (2001), Gwynn garnered 97.6 percent (532 of the 545) Hall of Fame votes cast by the Baseball Writers of America; you can only imagine what the recalcitrants were thinking.

"I never saw Ted Williams, Stan Musial or Joe DiMaggio," Rettenmund said, "but I've seen and studied everyone since and Tony's right there with the best of them. If you want a consistent hitter, you have to have a consistent person and he's certainly that.

"But beyond that, I'll give an example of how he's got every phase of the game covered. One day we're sitting in the dugout in a game against Atlanta and he says to anyone listening, 'Next time you're on second base against Greg Maddux, just take off for third. He looks back [from the stretch position], but he doesn't see you.' I don't know how many times we stole third successfully before Maddux finally corrected himself."

Since retiring, Tony Gwynn has taken up coaching baseball at his alma mater, San Diego State, and the team plays in Tony Gwynn Stadium, a $4 million present from Padres owner John Moores. That's how much they think about him there. ☐

WITH MORE THAN 40 YEARS OF EXPERIENCE IN THE NEWSPAPER BUSINESS, PHIL JACKMAN IS AN AWARD-WINNING SPORTSWRITER AND A MEMBER OF THE BASEBALL WRITERS' ASSOCIATION OF AMERICA.

It was the summer of 1983 and Tony Gwynn was struggling at the plate. He felt he had to do something to avoid being sent back to the minor leagues.

Gwynn had made his major league debut for San Diego in 1982, batting a respectable .289. He played winter ball in Puerto Rico after the season to polish his skills, but suffered a fractured wrist in December. The injury delayed his return to the Padres until late June of 1983 and now he wasn't hitting.

Gwynn decided to have his wife, Alicia, tape the television games while he was on the road so he could study his at-bats.

"When I got home and reviewed the tapes I could tell immediately what I was doing wrong," he said. "I was pulling off the ball and it was apparent to me from

Topps Gum offered new clients to their baseball cards a choice of $500 or a videotape machine. Gwynn took the machine and used it the entire season. "I took a lot of grief from other players for bringing this bulky, extra suitcase full of video equipment on the airplanes, but the video helped me do what I needed to do," he said.

In light of his success, it would seem other players would join Gwynn's videotape adventures, but none did.

In the late '80s, Sony came out with a portable, battery-powered video recorder that used much smaller tapes.

"I could use special cords to hook up the recorder to a television set in the clubhouse and record the games," Gwynn said. "Back in my hotel room I would dub my at-bats from the game on to another tape in a second recorder. This way I was

CAPTAIN VIDEO

By | Bob Chandler

watching the tape."

Batting just .233 at the time, Gwynn adjusted his swing and went on a hitting rampage. He averaged .333 the rest of the season to finish with a .309 average. He had one stretch in which he batted safely in 39 of 41 games, including a career-high 25-game streak. For the rest of his 20-year career, Gwynn would not bat under .309.

He became a believer in the value of videotape.

Gwynn's wife could record the telecasts of the road games, but the Padres televised very few home games in 1983.

"I went to the Jumbotron staff and got copies of the scoreboard replays, but the camera angles were not very good," Gwynn said. "There was no view from center field and the best shot of the hitters was from behind home plate."

Still, he spent all winter studying the tapes and working out every day to prepare for the 1984 season.

How did Gwynn do in 1984? He won the first of his eight batting titles with a .351 average, collecting a league-high 213 hits. In 606 at-bats, he struck out only 23 times. When asked the secret to his hitting success, Gwynn responded, "I just see the ball, hit the ball and run like hell."

Actually, there was a lot more to it than that.

getting the telecast coverage of the game with a lot more and better camera angles."

The recorder was small enough that Gwynn could actually watch replays during flights between cities.

"In addition to my at-bats, I studied the umpires, catchers and pitchers," he said. "Umpires are human and they all have slightly different strike zones. I learned which ones extend the strike zone, which ones call the high strike and so forth. I didn't complain to them about their strike zones, I just adjusted my strike zone to fit what they were calling. It really wasn't a problem for me, swinging at pitches a few inches outside or whatever."

"I learned which catchers set their target outside the strike zone," Gwynn said. "If the umpire is giving them the strike, they move the mitt out a little more. I always felt it was up to me to adjust. The Atlanta Braves catchers did that a lot for Tom Glavine and Greg Maddux. When Tony Pena was in Pittsburgh, he set up unusually low and frequently got the low strike called.

"Also, some catchers have what I call quiet feet or heavy feet. Some set their target early, others at the last second. If a catcher has heavy feet, I can hear him move behind me and I

– Captain Video –

can usually tell if he's setting up outside or inside. Gary Carter was a catcher who had quiet feet. I had a hard time knowing where he was setting up."

In Montreal one night, Carter was catching Charlie Lea, who had terrific stuff that game. "Carter decided to mess with my mind by telling me what pitch was coming and he was telling me the truth," Gwynn said. "I admit he was getting to me and we actually had an argument at home plate. ... I went 0-for-4, so you can chalk that one up to Carter."

Gwynn stewed about Carter that night and during the next game told him, "'Gary, you can say whatever you want. I'm blocking you out and not paying any attention.' I went 2-for-4 versus Bill Gullickson. Call it a draw between me and Carter. He's the only catcher in my career who tried that tactic."

Obviously, Gwynn spent a lot of time studying pitchers and their tendencies. "Pitchers who could hide the ball well gave me the most trouble," he said. "Randy Johnson and Omar Olivares are two that come immediately to mind. I concentrated hard on seeing the ball out of the pitcher's hand. It makes sense, the sooner I could identify the pitch, the more time I had to put a good swing on the ball."

Current Padres broadcaster Mark Grant was a major league pitcher who would frequently pitch batting practice to Gwynn when both were Padres. "Tony could recognize what pitch I was throwing when he saw my grip during the delivery," Grant said. "He would call slider, change, fastball, whatever, and then usually hit the ball hard somewhere."

Gwynn remembered a game against Pittsburgh in which he reached base on a single. Willie Stargell was the Pirates' first baseman.

"Tony, are you afraid of the fastball?" Stargell asked.

Gwynn wanted to know the reason for the question.

"You're lunging at the ball," Stargell said.

Gwynn checked his tapes that night and, sure enough, he was lunging. "The video helped me understand my need to stay back, get my front foot down, be in an athletic position and avoid my top hand rolling over," Gwynn said. "Stargell

could see I wasn't doing that."

The videotape confirmed it.

In the late '80s, Gwynn was so sold on the value of video equipment, he made a pitch to Padres general manager Jack McKeon. McKeon was old school and turned down Gwynn's request to purchase video equipment for the team.

"Nobody uses that stuff but you," Gwynn remembers McKeon arguing. So Gwynn ended up purchasing $100,000 of equipment, which he had installed in the clubhouse.

However, it turned out McKeon was right. Gwynn was the only Padre consistently using video.

Eventually, McKeon was replaced by Joe McIlvaine as GM and Gwynn talked him into hiring a part-time operator for the video equipment. Mike Howder worked at a San Diego TV station. During Gwynn's earlier use of video, Howder had helped provide tapes of his at-bats.

Howder was available during games and could provide immediate video of players' at-bats during the game. An infielder named Quilvio Veras was among the first players to take advantage. Later, team stars Greg Vaughn, Steve Finley and Ken Caminiti started to use the video and all were performing well. That seemed to bring the rest of the team into the fold.

Howder was still used only during home games until Gwynn talked management into taking him along on two important road trips.

"The Padres won 19 of 22 games during the two trips and general manager Kevin Towers decided it would be a good idea to have me travel full time," Howder said.

Now, all major league teams have top video equipment and it's common for a video man to make road trips.

Completely confident with his video work by 1997, Gwynn won his eighth and final batting title at the age of 37. In his opinion, he saved the best for last.

"It was my most complete season," Gwynn said. □

BOB CHANDLER IS SAN DIEGO'S LONGEST RUNNING SPORTSCASTER, HAVING STARTED HIS CAREER IN 1961. CHANDLER WAS A PLAY-BY-PLAY BROADCASTER FOR OVER 30 YEARS WITH THE SAN DIEGO PADRES AND HAS KNOWN TONY GWYNN SINCE COVERING HIS COLLEGE CAREER.

In a salute to broadcaster Marv Albert, the *New York Times* pays tribute in part by comparing the famed NBA play-by-play voice to a man who distinguished himself on another sporting landscape.

Albert's typical post-broadcast routine, writes Bryan Curtis in the *Times* on March 4, 2007, is to "[watch] a DVD of the broadcast in his hotel room, searching for hoary clichés – 'He shoots the J; Their backs are against the wall' – that make him sound like a poseur. It is reminiscent of late-career Tony Gwynn scrutinizing

to square up a baseball with a smaller bat."

"I think Tony helped change how players look at their bats," said longtime Padres equipment manager and director of team travel Brian Prilaman. "I don't think guys started using short and light bats until they saw how much success Tony had with it."

Prilaman recalled the ongoing relationship Gwynn cultivated with the Louisville Slugger company in Kentucky.

"He was one of those guys who made the effort to come to the factory," said Chuck Schupp, director of pro

BAT LOUDLY, CARRY A LITTLE STICK

By | Mike Lurie

tapes of his swing, and just as unnecessary."

And so it is, documented in the nation's newspaper of record: Tony Gwynn, a definition of batting excellence. More importantly, a standard for the painstaking process needed to achieve it.

While Gwynn scrutinized tapes of his swing in the literal sense, he also thought relentlessly about his swing and how to improve it.

That process began with a conscious decision he made early in his professional career.

As he transitioned from the aluminum bats he used at San Diego State to the wooden bats mandatory for professional ballplayers, Gwynn purposely chose a bat that was not only lightweight, but vertically challenged: 32 1/2 inches, about two inches shorter than the average. Typically, Gwynn's bat weighed 31 ounces, an ounce or so less than most.

"The reason why I used a short bat was control," Gwynn said. "In college, I swung a 32-inch bat, which in that era was unheard of because guys wanted to get whip. They wanted to get torque. And for me, it was just easier

baseball sales and promotions at Louisville Slugger. "For the players who come here, they get to see every step in the process.

"Not many players can do that, especially because there isn't a major league club in Louisville. But when a player can stop in, they can talk to the guys who make the bats. That's a good interaction to have. He made that effort and was just an easy person to work with."

Said Prilaman: "Tony liked the grain to be wide on his bat and I would guess II out of his I2 bats would be that way. The reason for that, I believe, is that we took a trip down to Louisville and had a good day talking with all the guys doing the lathe work and with the rest of their employees. After that, his bats were incredible."

The size of Gwynn's bat drew the attention, later in Gwynn's career, of another San Diego hitting legend.

It happened at the 1992 All-Star Game in San Diego, a chance meeting with native son Ted Williams.

"He had his entourage there and his security guards and he was on the third base line," Gwynn said. "So I just walked over and introduced myself. I happened to have

– Bat Loudly, Carry A Little Stick –

my bat in my hands. He said, 'Is that what you swing?' And I said, 'Yes, sir.'"

You carry a little diamond-cred when you are Ted Williams, the last .400 hitter in major league history, a man considered by many to be the greatest hitter of all time – inclusive of his heroic service (and missed at-bats) as an Air Force pilot during two wars.

When Ted Williams spoke, Tony Gwynn listened.

"I handed the bat to him and I think he was shocked with how small it was. Then he picked it up and started picking his teeth with it," Gwynn said.

Entering the 1992 season, Gwynn had finished with as high a batting average as .370 (1987) and never finished a year below .309 after his rookie season. But he was always tinkering.

"From '92 on, I became a more difficult out. I had just a little bit longer bat with better plate coverage," Gwynn said. "And I wasn't afraid of letting go if they came inside."

The man in uniform working most consistently with Gwynn on these adaptations was former Baltimore Orioles outfielder Merv Rettenmund, now the Padres' hitting coach.

EVERYTHING ABOUT TONY GWYNN'S SWING WAS A PERFECT MATCH FOR HIS SMALL BAT.

Rettenmund was well aware that Gwynn's bat was unusually small. However, to Rettenmund, the size of Gwynn's bat was just a part of what made him unique.

"The size of a hitter's bat really should be determined by what type of swing he has," Rettenmund said. He thought of former teammates in Baltimore, during the Orioles' glory days: first baseman Boog Powell, catcher Elrod Hendricks. Both used an unusually long bat. It matched their long, sweeping strokes.

Everything about Gwynn's swing was a perfect match for his small bat. The swing was compact, precise and most of all, a testament to tempo.

"He had great rhythm. You have to be able to recognize pitches and he waited for the ball so well," Rettenmund said. "He had this ability to let the pitch come to him.

Routinely he was hitting pitches six to eight inches off the plate. To do that, you've got to have perfect timing. He could focus on a pitcher's hand and time his swing on the pitcher's release point."

With that theory in mind, it's no wonder that the one pitcher who gave Gwynn trouble was a 6-foot-11 left-hander whose control could be unpredictable. Randy Johnson's release point was hard for Gwynn to assess.

Rettenmund notes that Gwynn truly became a fastball hitter during the final five years of his career. And with that transition, Gwynn – small bat and all – remained one step ahead.

"Of course, like so many other things in baseball, pitchers were slow to adjust to that," Rettenmund said.

It was during this final phase of Gwynn's career – New Testament Gwynn, if you will – that he passed the 3,000-hit plateau on Aug. 6, 1999.

Toward that destination, it's back to the *New York Times* and a conversation Gwynn engaged in with another member of the Hall of Fame, longtime baseball writer Murray Chass. It was late April of that '99 season and the Padres were in New York to face the Mets. Gwynn had 2,957 hits at the time of the conversation.

"I've had a passion to go out and play and do the things that I felt I could do," Gwynn told Chass. "Even today, that hasn't changed. I still have passion for the game. I still love to prepare and do all the other stuff I do."

He didn't have to increase the size of his bat by much, even after those talks with Ted Williams. The bat's light weight lent itself perfectly to Gwynn's compact swing and his ability to adjust to a pitch while it was in flight. Short bat and all, he was armed to work matters to his advantage. ☐

A LONGTIME SPORTSWRITER FOR NEWSPAPERS AND THE WEB, MIKE LURIE IS CURRENTLY A SPORTS REPORTER ON WYPR RADIO AND WORKS IN INSTITUTIONAL ADVANCEMENT AT UMBC.

om Glavine doesn't remember the year, but said it really didn't matter because this at-bat was like so many of his match-ups with Tony Gwynn – but even more so.

The New York Mets' crafty left-hander, who will someday join Gwynn in Cooperstown, smiled at the mention of the batsman's name.

Adversaries for so long – save brief respites as teammates on the National League All-Star teams – Glavine relished talking of Gwynn and did so in a tone that echoed equal parts respect and awe.

"It was in Atlanta and it was one of those prolonged at-bats he always had," Glavine said. "I had him 0-2,

you did, he always had an answer for it."

During those All-Star Game breaks, did Glavine and Gwynn ever talk about that at-bat? About any of their match-ups?

"We talked a little bit," Glavine said. "But, he was pretty humble when it came to talking about himself. There was no bravado about him. I don't think he needed to talk about himself. What he did spoke for itself."

Glavine said scouting reports were next to useless on Gwynn. Scouting reports denote patterns and trends and there was little predictability about Gwynn.

"He could handle hard stuff and he could handle off-speed stuff," Glavine said. "If you threw it off the

THE TOUGHEST OUT

By | John Delcos

but he battled back. He kept fouling them off, one right after another. He just got a piece of a few of them to stay alive."

After the count reached full, Glavine threw four straight fastballs, but Gwynn fought them off and the at-bat dragged on like an Academy Awards acceptance speech.

After a couple of changeups, the pitch count reached double figures when Glavine decided what he was doing wasn't working and he needed a different approach.

"I hadn't thrown him a curveball the entire time," Glavine said. "I threw it and – bam! – he hit a line drive for a hit.

"I thought to myself, 'There's no way he could be looking for that pitch.' But, that's him. That's what made him such a great hitter. He had such great plate coverage and he stayed with the pitch.

"There's no question he's the most complete hitter I ever saw. There were other guys who hit for more power, but he was the whole package. He was frustrating to pitch against because no matter what

outside corner he'd go that way. If you threw it inside he could pull you. So, the joke was to throw it down the middle and hope he'd get himself out."

Did that work?

"No," said Glavine, who carved out a large portion of his near 300 victories as a control pitcher living on the outside corner. Gwynn was tough for him because he didn't try to pull the ball and was content to slap a pitch into left.

However...

"If you went inside and didn't get it in far enough, he could turn on it and pull it out of the park," Glavine said.

While Gwynn was able to adjust at the plate, so too could Glavine on the mound, and with the Mets he has been throwing his curveball more on the inside corner.

It was a pitch he didn't throw to Gwynn.

"I would be interested to see what he would do with that pitch now," Glavine said. "I wish I could find that out, but I never will."

Odds are, Gwynn probably would have adjusted,

– The Toughest Out –

because that's what he did. That's what the great ones always do.

When NFL defenses tried to take away the long ball, Joe Montana would pick them apart short. When NBA defenses stacked to take away the drive, Michael Jordan would take the jumper or dish off with the pass.

Gwynn was never greedy at the plate, said Arizona Diamondbacks pitcher Randy Johnson, another who'll run into him one summer at Cooperstown.

"Tony had such a good approach to hitting." Johnson said. "He took what you would give him. If you pitched him away, he'd go with it. If you pitched him in, he would pull it. He had such good plate coverage and knowledge of the strike zone that you couldn't fool him."

Johnson throws classic high heat that reaches into the high 90s. He likes to climb the ladder with a hitter, starting low and working his way up the strike zone.

Johnson said Gwynn doesn't like the ball high, hard and in, which is the case for all left-handed hitters because of their swings. Even so, there was no guarantee that would work with Gwynn.

"Left-handed hitters don't like the ball there," Johnson said. "But, Tony was so good that when you threw that pitch to him he would just get a piece of it to stay alive. He'd keep doing that until you made a mistake."

Johnson lumps Gwynn in with Wade Boggs and Paul Molitor as complete hitters; they had the ability to hit for power, but were more dangerous because

they would always get the bat on the ball.

It happened to Johnson in a playoff game while he was with Houston. It was scoreless when Gwynn came to the plate with a runner on.

Johnson came at Gwynn with that big, sweeping delivery of his, the one that caused palpitations for John Kruk at the 1993 All-Star Game in Baltimore.

Johnson had been working Gwynn with fastballs, but what came this time was a nasty slider.

"His butt went toward the first base dugout and his bat went the other way," Johnson said. "He got it and knocked it down the line."

And in came the winning run.

Johnson said pitching to Gwynn, Molitor and Boggs was like playing cards; they'd discard what they didn't like until they got what they wanted.

"They would tire you out," Johnson said. "They would just keep the at-bat going. If the pitches were borderline, Tony could foul them off at will. You throw him eight, nine, 10 pitches; he's seen everything you have. He's just waiting for you to make a mistake. There aren't any hitters like that today."

Both Johnson and Glavine said today's batters swing for power, which plays into their hands.

"I would much rather face a power hitter than a guy like Tony," Johnson said. "Power hitters are more one-dimensional. They have one way to beat you. But Tony could beat you in a lot of ways. He'd wait for you to make a mistake, but if you didn't he'd take the walk."

The classic thinking was that if a hitter like Ted

– The Toughest Out –

Williams or Pete Rose wouldn't swing at a pitch, then it had to be a ball.

"You weren't going to get the close calls on him," Mets closer Billy Wagner said. "The umpires had so much respect of his knowledge of the strike zone that if he wasn't swinging it wasn't a strike."

Former Mets pitcher Ron Darling faced Gwynn earlier in his career, and said he was a different player before having injury problems.

"His body belied how really a good athlete he was," Darling said. "He was a great fielder. His job was to get on base and when he did, he was an excellent base runner. He could steal a base when he had to and he would always take the extra base.

"People know him as a great hitter, but he was a great player. And he was a superstar who was sincerely a nice guy."

Darling, like Glavine, Johnson and Wagner before him, joked about throwing it down the middle.

Former Los Angeles Dodgers catcher Paul Lo Duca, now with the Mets, said there was truth in humor.

Gwynn's plate coverage and adaptability made it virtually impossible to come up with a pitching game plan against him. He hit high and low, in and out, soft and hard.

What then?

"We didn't have a game plan against him," said Lo Duca, who used to sit in on the pre-series Padres-Dodgers pitching meetings.

"The one thing you didn't want to do is throw him the same pitch twice in a row. You might be able to get him out with soft stuff one time, but you'd better not throw it the next time. If you threw him the same pitch again or if you'd make a mistake, he would make you pay."

Which is something Tony Gwynn did to pitchers more than 3,000 times. □

JOHN DELCOS CURRENTLY COVERS THE METS FOR GANNETT NEWSPAPERS IN WESTCHESTER, N.Y.

G

"THERE'S NO QUESTION HE'S THE MOST COMPLETE HITTER I EVER SAW."

– Tom Glavine –

THE 3,000 HIT CLUB

	Player	YRS	AVG	H		Player	YRS	AVG	H
1	Pete Rose	1963-1986	.303	4,256	14	Cal Ripken Jr.	1981-2001	.276	3,184
2	Ty Cobb	1905-1928	.367	4,191	15	George Brett	1973-1993	.305	3,154
3	Hank Aaron	1954-1976	.305	3,771	16	Paul Waner	1926-1945	.333	3,152
4	Stan Musial	1941-1963	.331	3,630	17	Robin Yount	1974-1993	.285	3,142
5	Tris Speaker	1907-1928	.345	3,514	18	Tony Gwynn	1982-2001	.338	3,141
6	Carl Yastrzemski	1961-1983	.285	3,419	19	Dave Winfield	1973-1995	.283	3,110
7	Cap Anson	1871-1897	.333	3,418	20	Rickey Henderson	1979-2003	.279	3,055
8	Honus Wagner	1897-1917	.327	3,415	21	Rod Carew	1967-1985	.328	3,053
9	Paul Molitor	1978-1998	.306	3,319	22	Lou Brock	1961-1979	.293	3,023
10	Eddie Collins	1906-1930	.333	3,315	23	Rafael Palmeiro	1986-2005	.288	3,020
11	Willie Mays	1951-1973	.302	3,283	24	Wade Boggs	1982-1999	.328	3,010
12	Eddie Murray	1977-1997	.287	3,255	25	Al Kaline	1953-1974	.297	3,007
13	Nap Lajoie	1896-1916	.338	3,242	26	Roberto Clemente	1955-1972	.317	3,000

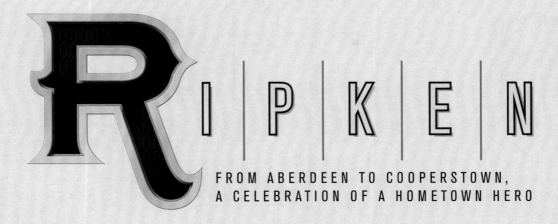

"**H**it, hit, hit" replied probable Hall of Fame relief pitcher Rich "Goose" Gossage when asked what came to mind when the newly-elected Hall of Famer Tony Gwynn was mentioned.

"Tony will go down as one of the best professional hitters in the history of baseball," Gossage continued. "If you open the dictionary to 'hitter,' you should find a picture of Gwynn. In fact, I played for some great teams in Chicago, Pittsburgh and New York, but the best 1-2 tandem at the top of the batting order was Alan Wiggins and Tony Gwynn in 1984 when San Diego won its first pennant."

For the record, Wiggins stole 70 bases that season and

his work. I learned a lot and it was unbelievable watching the respect he got around the league."

Incidentally, after watching Gwynn get hit No. 3,000, Nevin doubled him home.

— — — — — — — — — — — — — — — — — — — —

Two former major league catchers noticed more than Gwynn's hitting. Norm Sherry is a one-time major league manager who was the pitching coach for the Padres when Gwynn first came to the major leagues in 1982. Terry Kennedy was the Padres' starting catcher. Sherry and Kennedy both pointed out Gwynn's early deficiencies as an outfielder and how hard he worked to improve.

"Tony was a below average outfielder with a weak arm when

TONY THE TEAMMATE

By | Bob Chandler

scored 106 runs. Gwynn stole 33 bases, won his first batting title with a .351 average and led the National League with 213 hits. When Wiggins was on first base, opponents so feared his stolen base abilities that they threw Gwynn lots of fastballs. Gwynn batted .412 with Wiggins on first.

— — — — — — — — — — — — — — — — — — — —

Current Padres relief ace Trevor Hoffman remembers Gwynn's batting ability.

"I came to the Padres in June of 1993 and witnessed Tony hitting .402 in over 500 at-bats from July of 1993 to July of 1994," he said.

Major League Baseball went on strike in mid-August of 1994. Gwynn was batting .394 at the time and many, including Gwynn, believe he would have batted .400 if the season had played to its conclusion. The last major league player to accomplish a .400 average was another San Diegan, Ted Williams (.406 in 1941 with the Red Sox).

— — — — — — — — — — — — — — — — — — — —

Slugger Phil Nevin came to the Padres in a 1999 trade and was waiting to bat when Gwynn collected hit No. 3,000 in Montreal. "One of the reasons I was thrilled to be traded to San Diego was the opportunity of watching Tony Gwynn hit," he said. "I also wanted to watch how a Hall of Famer goes about

he first joined the team," Kennedy said. "But he learned how to charge the ball and come up throwing to improve his arm and worked so hard on his defense that in 1986 he won a Gold Glove." Gwynn finished his career with five Gold Gloves for defensive excellence.

— — — — — — — — — — — — — — — — — — — —

Gwynn's first major league manager, Dick Williams, guided the Padres to their first pennant in 1984 and Tony was an integral part of that team.

"I can't say enough good things about Gwynn," Williams said. "He always played hard for me. I remember him using the whole field as a hitter. I also wanted him to lose some weight, but it seemed the more pounds he put on, the more batting titles he won."

Gwynn also learned a valuable lesson from Williams in July 1984. "I hit a routine grounder to second base and didn't run hard to first," he said. "Cincinnati's Ron Oester bobbled the ball but was still able to turn the double play. Williams immediately took me out of the lineup and put Bobby Brown in right field. Later in the game Brown messed up a fly ball and we lost."

When Williams called him into his office the next day, Gwynn was upset about being removed from the game.

– Tony The Teammate –

The manager asked, "Do you know why I took you out of yesterday's game?"

Gwynn answered that he did.

"You know you cost us the game," Williams said.

"How did I cost us the game?" Gwynn responded. "You took me out."

"Because I had to put Brown in right field," Williams snapped back. "And he messed up the play. If you had been out there, you'd have caught the ball."

It's a lesson Gwynn now tries to teach to his players as coach of San Diego State's baseball team.

Bruce Bochy was Gwynn's teammate in the '80s, a Padres coach for two seasons and the manager in the final seven seasons of Gwynn's career.

"It was a privilege to manage Tony," he said. "His personality never changed from his early days with the Padres until the end of his career. He was usually the first player in the clubhouse and always made himself available to other players and the media."

It was no fluke that Tony's locker was next to the manager's office. "I talked baseball with Tony all the time," Bochy said. "I picked his mind about many different subjects and there's no doubt he helped me become a better manager."

Bochy is now the manager of the San Francisco Giants.

Current Padres manager Buddy Black was a teammate of Gwynn's in the late '70s at San Diego State.

"I remember mostly his athleticism, his great hand-eye coordination and how he played with so much joy," Black said.

Padres fans eagerly anticipated the arrival of Gwynn in the major leagues. Based on his basketball and baseball exploits at San Diego State, he was already a well-known San Diego sports figure. When he became the Padres' third round draft choice in June 1981, his minor league accomplishments garnered unprecedented interest.

Gwynn led the Rookie Northwest League with a .331

batting average and was selected league MVP that first summer of 1981. Anticipation increased when he moved up to Double-A Amarillo in the Texas League for the final three weeks of the season and hit .462 in 91 at-bats.

In 1982, a little more than a year after signing his professional contract, Gwynn was batting .328 for the Padres' Triple-A affiliate in Hawaii when his call to the major leagues came. He arrived in San Diego on July 19, 1982 and was immediately inserted into the starting lineup by Williams. Gwynn played in center field and batted fifth in the order against the Philadelphia Phillies.

In his first at-bat, Gwynn hit a sacrifice fly to center field. He lined out to shortstop in his second at-bat and struck out in his third. In the eighth inning, though, Gwynn collected the first of his 3,141 hits – a double to left field. In the last inning, he rapped out his second base hit, a clean single, eliciting a rousing ovation from the 34,433 in attendance, an audience that sensed something special about this debut.

Naturally, not every teammate loved Gwynn. Perhaps his biggest adversary was slugger Jack Clark during the 1990 season. Clark felt Gwynn was a selfish player and a team meeting was called when the club was in New York. Gwynn remembered that Clark started the meeting by throwing a cup of root beer across the clubhouse. Current Padres broadcaster Mark Grant was a pitcher on that team and confirmed the cup exploded when it hit between his legs.

Clark pointed a finger at Gwynn and said, "You're the problem on this team; you're a selfish son of a bitch!"

Gwynn had other ideas and admits now, "I said some things to Jack I probably shouldn't have."

Soon, they were nose to nose and a fight almost ensued. It's Tony's opinion that Clark felt Gwynn received too much attention for a player who was not a "game-changer." Clark objected to Gwynn's dragging a bunt when runners were on first and second and nobody out. It was his opinion that Gwynn was trying to protect his batting average by either getting a bunt single or credit for a sacrifice.

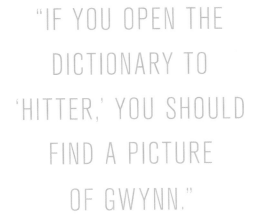

"IF YOU OPEN THE DICTIONARY TO 'HITTER,' YOU SHOULD FIND A PICTURE OF GWYNN."

– Goose Gossage –

– Tony The Teammate –

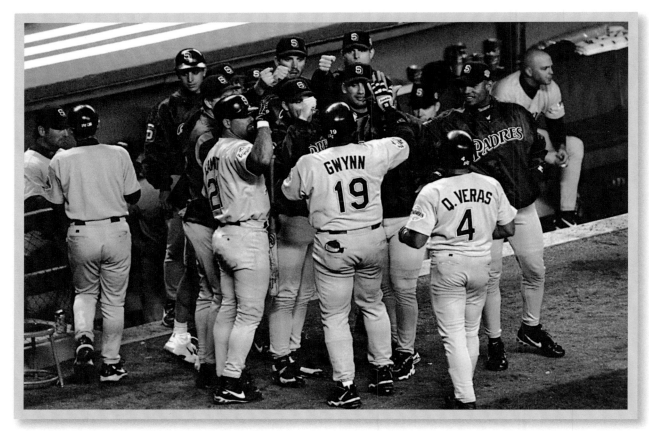

TONY GWYNN RECEIVES CONGRATULATIONS FROM HIS TEAMMATES AFTER HITTING A HOME RUN DURING
GAME 1 OF THE 1998 WORLD SERIES AGAINST THE NEW YORK YANKEES ON OCT. 17, 1998.

Tony felt he was helping the team by advancing the runners for the "game-changers" – Clark and Joe Carter. He was simply playing the Dick Williams/Jack McKeon style of baseball.

Nevertheless, for the rest of the season, Gwynn never bunted in that situation again. He tried to drive the ball and saw his batting average drop to .309, even though he drove in 10 more runs than in 1989.

Gwynn always credited Steve Garvey with setting an example for dealing with the media. In 1983, Garvey was an icon who had signed with the Padres as a free agent following a stellar career with the Los Angeles Dodgers. Garvey credited Gwynn "as being very coachable. A good athlete with tremendous instincts."

He compared Tony to Cal Ripken, two outstanding players who played their entire careers with one team. Garvey emphasized to Gwynn that reporters were the players' conduit to the fans and that it doesn't take a lot of effort to cooperate.

Gwynn became one of the most media-cooperative players in the history of the game.

The final word on Gwynn is supplied by former teammate and coach Tim Flannery. "The Padres were in Cincinnati trailing the Reds 2-0 in the late innings when rain suspended the game until the next day," Flannery said. "Tony Gwynn was the hitter and the Padres had two runners on base."

"The pitcher was Derek Lilliquist," Gwynn said. "He had me down in the count 1-2 and it was the first time I ever had 24 hours to think about what pitch he would throw." Flannery was the third base coach and he recalls Gwynn telling him, "Flan, he's going to throw me a slider and I'm going to drive the ball to left-center. Be ready to wave those runners home."

The pitch was indeed a slider and Flannery waved the runs in as Gwynn cruised to second with a stand-up double to left-center. ☐

BOB CHANDLER IS SAN DIEGO'S LONGEST RUNNING SPORTSCASTER, HAVING STARTED HIS CAREER IN 1961. CHANDLER WAS A PLAY-BY-PLAY BROADCASTER FOR MORE THAN 30 YEARS WITH THE SAN DIEGO PADRES AND HAS KNOWN TONY GWYNN SINCE COVERING HIS COLLEGE CAREER.

PLAYING THROUGH PAIN

By | John Maffei

ony Gwynn threw up his hands, leaned back in his chair and roared the rich Tony Gwynn laugh that seems to come from his shoes.

"Has there ever been a bigger contrast between two guys going into the Hall of Fame than between Cal Ripken and myself?" Gwynn asked.

Ripken is Major League Baseball's "Iron Man," playing a record 2,632 consecutive games. He went 17 years before making a trip to the disabled list.

Gwynn – the eight-time National League batting champion – had 10 knee surgeries, four of those of the major variety. Over the last part of his career, he was held together by surgical sutures, knee drains and deep-tissue rubs.

Injuries to his fingers, wrist, knees and Achilles tendon cost Gwynn about 500 games – the equivalent of three full seasons.

He finished his brilliant 20-year career, all in the uniform of the San Diego Padres, with 3,141 hits and a .338 batting average.

Had he been healthy, had he not had to play the last 10 years of his career on one leg, he might have attained his goal of catching the great Hank Aaron's 3,771 career hits, third on baseball's all-time list.

"That would have been nice, but you can't worry about numbers," said Gwynn, who recently finished his fourth season as baseball coach at San Diego State University, the school where he starred in basketball

"I CAN'T TELL YOU WHAT THE DOCTORS MEANT TO ME. ... THEY PIECED ME BACK TOGETHER."

– Tony Gwynn –

and baseball. "I'm not going to look back and say, 'If only this had happened.'

"Every injury I had, happened on the field. I missed a lot of games, but there were times I shouldn't have played. I played with a bad Achilles and shouldn't have played the second half of the season. But I did. I tore knee cartilage and shouldn't have played, but I did. I sucked it up.

"The way I looked at it was: 'Was I productive?' The answer was always yes."

For a good part of Gwynn's career, the job of holding him together fell to trainer Todd Hutcheson.

"We did things to make Tony feel comfortable," Hutcheson said. "And at times we had to be creative. There were compression sleeves, pumps and plenty of soft tissue massages."

In 1990, Gwynn fractured his right index finger trying to make a catch against the wall in Atlanta. Hutcheson and his staff designed a plastic cup that was fixed onto Gwynn's glove, allowing him to play.

In 1995, Gwynn fouled a ball off his right big toe, fracturing it. The training staff designed a cover for Gwynn's shoe that allowed him to play.

"Tony wanted to be in the lineup and we wanted to give him the best opportunity to play every game," Hutcheson said. "He didn't like sitting. That was difficult at times because we knew he was going to go out there, no matter what.

"And with Tony, it was kind of a Catch-22. The

– Playing Through Pain –

better he hit, the harder it was to keep him off the field. The better he hit, the more he ran, the more pounding his knees and Achilles took.

"And the old artificial turf fields killed him. All that pounding, all that stress accumulates. Tony was injured a lot and missed a lot of games. But people don't realize that he played through a ton of crap."

Gwynn's first major knee surgery was in late 1991, costing him the final 21 games of that season. He had knee surgeries again in 1992, 1993 and 2000 all performed by Drs. Cliff Colwell, Jan Fronk and Steve Copp.

The left knee – the back leg for a left-handed hitter – was the hardest for him to deal with.

"I can't tell you what the doctors meant to me," Gwynn said. "They were all great. They pieced me back together. But I really enjoyed dealing with Dr. Copp. He was an athlete. He really laid things out for you. He gave you the who, what, where, when and how of every injury. And I loved his honesty."

In addition to being a Rhodes Scholarship finalist, the 6-foot-7 Copp was a two-time all-conference basketball player at San Diego State, twice leading the Aztecs into the NCAA tournament and finishing his career as the school's fifth all-time leading scorer.

He was drafted by the then-New Orleans Jazz, but opted to pursue his post-graduate studies.

"I enjoy working with all my patients, but as a former athlete, I really enjoy working with athletes," Copp said. "I knew Tony at San Diego State, then as a professional athlete. That was very important in our doctor-patient relationship.

"At first, his knee surgeries were pretty routine. Later, they were pretty bad. What people really didn't realize was that the Achilles injury was unusually bad. His career was definitely at risk."

Gwynn bounced back from that surgery and played in 149 games in 1997, setting career highs for hits (220), doubles (49), home runs (17) and RBIs (119). And he hit .372, winning the last of his batting titles.

"I rehabbed the Achilles for four months," Gwynn said. "I worked all winter to get it right. I reported early to spring training, as usual, and people were shocked. I just dealt with it."

Gwynn's weight was questioned late in his career.

In college, the 5-foot-11 Gwynn played at about 185 pounds. He was a quick point guard on the basketball team and is still the school's all-time leader in assists.

As he got older, he got bigger, but he said the weight led to success.

"Early in my career, I loved to run," said Gwynn, who had 319 career stolen bases, including a career-high 56 in 1987. "But I was hitting first or second, spots that

– Playing Through Pain –

allowed me to run. Later in my career, I moved down to third. That isn't a running spot. And when players hit 30, the run game usually slows down.

"As for the weight thing, I wouldn't be where I am today if I had continued to play at 185. As I got older, got smarter as a hitter, I found that I was very comfortable at 225-235. Hitting is all about balance, and I felt I had great balance at 225-235. And no, I don't feel that my weight led to injuries or made them worse."

Late in his career, Gwynn said the worst part of the injuries was getting fluid drained from his knee.

Hutcheson explained that the doctors and training staff usually tried to drain the fluid after a Sunday day game, especially if the team had Monday off. With a Tuesday night game, that allowed Gwynn nearly 48 hours of recovery time.

"I easily had 150-200 knee drains," Gwynn said. "They were painful, but you get used to it. That needle was real long and it was horrible. I was pretty grumpy when I went in, but the doctors did a good job of taking my mind off things. My knee would be the size of a grapefruit when I went in and in five minutes, it was back to normal size. I hated it, but I knew I'd feel better when it was over."

More than his weight, more than running the bases and playing on hard outfield surfaces, Gwynn believes his knee problems came from swinging the bat.

"People think I'm a natural hitter," Gwynn said. "That's not true. I had to work at my craft. I felt I had to take at least 100 swings a day to be a good hitter. I was certainly willing to work, but all that torque causes your knees to bark. At the end, I could have played another year or two, but I pulled a hamstring trying to compensate for my knees.

"And I knew Coach [Jim] Dietz was planning to retire at San Diego State. I wanted that job and it was a factor I couldn't control. I couldn't tell Coach Dietz to hang on while I kept playing.

"In 2001, we were playing in Pittsburgh and I started in right field. I hit a home run and a double. The next day, everything ached and I told myself, 'I can't do this anymore.'" ☐

JOHN MAFFEI IS A SPORTSWRITER AT THE NORTH COUNTY TIMES AND HAS COVERED THE PADRES SINCE 1978.

TONY GWYNN'S CAREER INJURIES

1983:	Fractured wrist in Puerto Rico Winter League and missed start of 1983 season.
1985:	Injured wrist in mid-season collision at home plate with Mike Scioscia of the Los Angeles Dodgers.
1988:	Had surgery on left wrist in March. Went on the 21-day disabled list in May.
1989:	Battled through wrist and Achilles injuries the second half of the season.
1990:	Missed 19 games with fractured right index finger.
1991:	Had surgery on left knee Sept. 16 and missed final 21 games of the season.
1992:	Fractured tip of right index finger. Sprained the medial collateral ligament of his left knee in San Francisco Sept. 8 and played just six innings the rest of the season. Had surgery Oct. 6.
1993:	Injured left knee in Atlanta Sept. 5 and had surgery Sept. 12.
1995:	Fouled ball off his right big toe Aug. 3 in San Francisco, causing a fracture.
1996:	Missed eight games with inflamed bursa sac in right heel. Went on DL July 2 with fraying of right Achilles and missed 30 games. Had surgery on right heel and Achilles after the season.
1998:	Missed 18 games with inflamed left Achilles.
1999:	Missed 44 games with strained left calf.
2000:	Had surgery on left knee in June to clean out small pieces of cartilage.

GROWING UP GWYNN

By | Tom Haudricourt

From the day he was born, Tony Gwynn Jr. was in sync with his future Hall of Fame dad.

Tony Jr. was born on Oct. 4, 1982 in Long Beach, Calif., one day after his father completed the first of his 20 seasons with the San Diego Padres. With the fortuitous timing of his son's birth, Gwynn did not have to miss a game during his rookie season.

"I don't know if it was planned but it ended up working out that way," Tony Jr. said with a laugh. "Actually, I was a month late. I was supposed to be born on Sept. 4."

It wasn't long before Tony Jr. was accompanying his father to the ballpark, where many of the Padres took him under their collective wings. But it wasn't until he was about 9 or 10 that the younger Gwynn figured out how lucky he was to grow up in that kind of atmosphere.

"I latched on to quite a few of my dad's teammates," he said. "I remember hanging out with John Kruk when I was real little. He was one of my best friends. Then it was Joe Carter, Sheff [Gary Sheffield], guys like that. It was one of those things where I didn't really ask to go. He'd just say, 'Do you want to go to the park today?' And I'd say, 'Yeah, I'll go.'"

Despite that early indoctrination to the game of

baseball, Tony Jr. was not pressured to follow in his dad's footsteps. As a youngster, he preferred basketball, a sport his father probably could have made a nice living in after a standout career at San Diego State University.

"My dad never forced baseball on me," Gwynn Jr. said. "Never. He didn't try to steer me away from it but he was never really vocal about baseball. He let me make that decision.

"I really liked to play basketball. And he was a lot tougher on me about basketball than he ever was about baseball. I can remember a couple of games in high school where I came home and he was upset with me. But with baseball I could go 0-for-20 and he wouldn't have any emotion."

Busy with his own career, Gwynn didn't get to see his son play much baseball at Poway High School. But once the Padres' season was done, he would attend every one of Tony Jr.'s basketball games.

Tony Jr. didn't play much baseball until his junior year. Still concentrating on basketball, he was about to give up on baseball when his father intervened.

"My dad said, 'You should have something to fall back on,'" Tony Jr. said. "I was ready to just play basketball. As it turned out, he was right."

Tony Jr. started to blossom on the diamond that

– Growing Up Gwynn –

year, batting .400. He was invited to play in the Area Code Games, a high school showcase attended by professional scouts from across the country. Suddenly, he began to realize that baseball might be the sport for him.

"That's when the light went on that maybe it was time to put basketball away and just play baseball," he said.

As Tony Jr. continued to hone his baseball skills as a senior, scholarship offers started to come in from top college programs. Shunning overtures from his dad's alma mater, he verbally committed to attend Cal State Fullerton.

About the same time, the elder Gwynn began to contemplate his retirement from the major leagues and San Diego State approached him about taking over the school's baseball program.

"He kind of pulled me aside and said, 'Coach [Jim] Dietz really wants me to take this job. I think I'm about ready to coach now,'" Tony Jr. said. "He won't admit to it but he was hurt that I chose Cal State Fullerton over San Diego State. I kind of sat on it for two days, then I called Coach [George] Horton at Fullerton and said I was thinking about changing my mind and going to San Diego State.

"He was good about it. He said, 'Playing for your dad is an opportunity you rarely get, so go ahead.'"

Gwynn, who served as San Diego State's hitting coach during his son's sophomore season, took over the head coaching reins the next year, 2003. For one fun-filled season, the steadily improving son got to play for his proud papa.

"It was awesome," Tony Jr. said. "It was the most time I ever spent with him. Even when he was the hitting coach, he wasn't there for all the games. He was still doing some broadcasting on the side.

"I wasn't going to put him in a position where people felt like he was giving me special treatment. I did my part, did everything I was supposed to do, so it wasn't even something that came up."

While most of Tony Jr.'s teammates were in awe of their famous coach, the son never thought much about that privilege. And if others expected him to be a chip off the old baseball block, Tony Jr. never felt pressure to step into those sizable cleats.

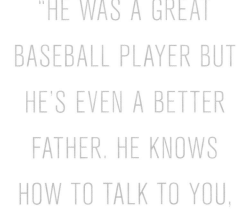

"HE WAS A GREAT BASEBALL PLAYER BUT HE'S EVEN A BETTER FATHER. HE KNOWS HOW TO TALK TO YOU, WHAT TO SAY."

– Tony Gwynn Jr. –

"I don't think I thought about that," he said. "I knew before I got to high school that if I was going to play baseball, I was going to have to separate what my dad did and what I did. You've got to come to that realization early, that there's only one Tony Gwynn."

As the 2003 major league draft approached, it became evident that Tony Jr. would go in an early round. As the first round passed and the second began the prospect of being selected by his father's team loomed large.

The Milwaukee Brewers went second in Round 2, two picks ahead of the Padres. If Tony Jr. was still on the board when San Diego's turn came, he would have most likely been tabbed.

"My uncle Chris was a scout for the Padres and he later told me they would have taken me," Tony Jr. said.

But the Brewers had other ideas. They selected Tony Jr., sparing him the pressure of having to follow in his father's footsteps in San Diego.

"It would have been a big issue for me to go to the Padres," Tony Jr. admitted. "It would have been a different beast, no doubt. But I had come to terms with it and would have been able to deal with it.

– Growing Up Gwynn –

"As it turned out, I was taken by the Brewers. I tell my parents all the time how blessed I am to be in an organization like this. I talk to friends who play baseball in other organizations and the teaching isn't there. In this organization, as hard as it is being a Hall of Famer's son, I've learned a lot about myself and the things I needed to do to be successful."

Tony Jr. was assigned to Single-A Beloit (Wis.), where he immediately bumped into the son of another famous major leaguer. Prince Fielder, son of feared slugger Cecil Fielder and the Brewers' first round pick in 2002, was about to embark on a season at Beloit in which he would bat .313 with 27 home runs and 112 RBIs, a performance that earned him Most Valuable Player honors in the Midwest League.

When Tony Jr. reported to manager Don Money's office, Fielder happened to be there, talking to the skipper. The affable first baseman immediately made Tony Jr. an offer he couldn't refuse.

"He said, 'Hey man, you want to stay with me?'" Tony Jr. said. "He said that right away, without hesitation. I said, 'Yeah, sure.' We hit it off right away."

Thus began a close friendship that soon would include second baseman Rickie Weeks, the Brewers' first round draft pick in '03. Tony Jr. already had established a relationship with Weeks during their days on the amateur baseball circuit and the Team USA tryouts.

Before long, the three teammates were inseparable. As sons of former big league stars, Fielder and Tony Jr. had plenty in common.

TONY GWYNN JR. WAS A FIRST TEAM ALL-AMERICAN IN 2003, WHILE HIS FATHER SERVED AS HEAD COACH AT SAN DIEGO STATE.

"I'm sure that had something to do with it," Tony Jr. said. "At the same time, Prince was just looking for somebody who could relate to him. It made my transition very easy."

The next season, the three amigos advanced to Double-A Huntsville. Fielder and Weeks continued to prosper but Tony Jr. struggled to adjust to the rigors of his first full professional season, finishing with a .243 batting average and 34 stolen bases in a league-leading 138 games.

In 2005, Fielder and Weeks were promoted to Triple-A Nashville and Tony Jr. was held back in Huntsville for another season. Initially, it was a painful parting, but Tony Jr. became more determined than ever to catch up.

"It was inevitable," Tony Jr. said. "Those guys had such a high ceiling and were so much further along than I was. I knew they were going to push Rickie, and Prince had a lot more professional experience than I had because he was drafted out of high school."

Tony Jr., a prototypical speedy leadoff hitter who bats from the left side, was already playing major league-quality defense in center field. All he needed to do was prove he could handle himself at the plate.

And he did exactly that. He raised his average to .271 in his second season at Huntsville, then moved on to Nashville in 2006. It was there he enjoyed a breakthrough campaign, batting .300 in 112 games with five triples, four homers, 42 RBIs and 30 stolen bases. Tony Jr. was rewarded with two stints with the

– Growing Up Gwynn –

Brewers, batting .260 in 32 games.

What was the key to that marked improvement between the 2005 and 2006 seasons? For one thing, a winter of detail-oriented work with his coach and father.

"I really started to get in my dad's head about anything I could think of," Tony Jr. said. "He was a great baseball player but he's even a better father. He knows how to talk to you, what to say.

"I looked at that offseason like I was going to war. I wasn't shaving or anything. I was just going to work, work, work. My dad was there, right by me. And he had other obligations as the head coach at San Diego State. It's just as important to him as me that I become a successful major league player."

Upon being summoned to the majors for the first time in 2006, Tony Jr. once again proved just how in sync he is with his father. On July 19 in San Francisco, he collected his first major league hit – a pinch-hit double off Giants reliever Brian Wilson. It came 24 years to the day after his father's first big-league hit – a double off Philadelphia's Sid Monge.

"That was spooky," Tony Jr. said. "It can't get any more similar than that. It was his third at-bat and my third at-bat. I don't know if it was the same count but I wouldn't be surprised if it was.

"When I got the hit, it still didn't dawn on me. When I got off the field, somebody said, 'Your dad got his first hit on the same day,' and I looked and it was on the scoreboard. That's pretty remarkable. Everything was lined up way too perfect for it not to be destiny or fate."

Good things continued to happen to the Gwynns over the winter. In November, Tony Jr. married longtime sweetheart Alyse. Then, in January, with family and friends gathered in expectation, the telephone call came with news that Tony Gwynn had been elected to the Hall of Fame.

"It was almost surreal," Tony Jr. said. "In all the years he played, I'm talking World Series and everything, I never saw this guy nervous. But I got there that morning and he was outside in the backyard, pacing back and forth, back and forth.

"He was visibly shaking. That day, I realized how big a deal it was. When he got the phone call, he started crying. I was in the kitchen and I came in

THE GWYNNS: A BASEBALL FAMILY

TONY GWYNN

- FULL NAME: Anthony Keith Gwynn
- BORN: May 9, 1960   MLB DEBUT: July 19, 1982
- Drafted by the San Diego Padres in the third round (No. 58 overall) of the 1981 MLB Draft.
- Over his 20-year career, Tony Gwynn batted .338 while amassing 3,141 hits in 9,288 at-bats.

CHRIS GWYNN

- FULL NAME: Christopher Karlton Gwynn
- BORN: Oct. 13, 1964   MLB DEBUT: Aug. 14, 1987
- Drafted by the Los Angeles Dodgers in the first round (No. 10 overall) of the 1985 MLB Draft.
- Over his 10-year career, Chris Gwynn batted .261 with 36 doubles and 118 RBIs in 599 games.

TONY GWYNN JR.

- FULL NAME: Anthony Keith Gwynn Jr.
- BORN: Oct. 4, 1982   MLB DEBUT: July 15, 2006
- Drafted by the Milwaukee Brewers in the second round (No. 39 overall) of the 2003 MLB Draft.
- In 2006, Tony Gwynn Jr. batted .260 in 77 at-bats over 32 games for the Milwaukee Brewers. He had two doubles, one triple, three stolen bases, four RBIs and five runs scored.

and gave him a big hug. He was crying but I was just smiling and laughing. It was a joyous occasion, a great moment for the entire family."

At the outset of spring training, Tony Jr. made sure to get permission from Milwaukee general manager Doug Melvin to attend the induction ceremonies in Cooperstown, N.Y., on July 29. But he might have messed up those plans by making the Brewers' big-league roster out of camp. □

TOM HAUDRICOURT COVERS THE MILWAUKEE BREWERS AND MAJOR LEAGUE BASEBALL FOR THE MILWAUKEE JOURNAL SENTINEL. WITH THE EXCEPTION OF A BRIEF PERIOD FROM 2002-03, HE HAS COVERED BASEBALL IN MILWAUKEE SINCE 1985.

San Diegans are a provincial lot.

It's what happens when you live in the shadow of the Los Angeles megaplex.

No matter how blue the waters of the Pacific and how wonderful the climate, San Diegans have always had something of a chip on our paradise.

You are with us, or . . .

Which is what makes Tony Gwynn special.

Gwynn was not raised a San Diegan. He chose to join us. And over the years, when greener pastures beckoned, Gwynn chose to remain a San Diegan.

Not just a Padre, mind you. A San Diegan.

"Very few athletes have had greater impact on their probably should be Bobby Meacham."

Now a Padres coach, the former Yankee infielder was being recruited by Dietz in the spring of 1978 when he noticed Gwynn walking down the hall of San Diego State's athletic department.

"I told Coach Dietz, 'Wow, I didn't know you had the best player in Southern California here,'" Meacham said. "Coach Dietz said, 'No, that's Tony Gwynn, he's a basketball player.' I said, 'That's Tony Gwynn, the best hitter I've ever seen.'"

And the rest is history.

Gwynn started playing baseball as well as basketball at San Diego State. And on June 9, 1981, the Gwynn

MR. SAN DIEGO

By | Bill Center

community than Tony Gwynn," Padres owner John Moores said several years ago in tribute to the Hall of Famer. "In truth, it is probably impossible to gauge the totality of Tony's contributions."

The year of Gwynn's induction into the Hall of Fame is also the 30th anniversary of his arrival in San Diego. Five years before he debuted with the Padres, Gwynn was making his mark on the San Diego sports scene.

A native of Long Beach who grew up a fan of the Los Angeles Dodgers, Gwynn came to San Diego because of his talents as a basketball player. He was recruited by San Diego State as a point guard and set school records for assists that still stand.

In fact, Gwynn's path to a baseball field in San Diego was anything but straight.

"When I arrived, I was playing for a basketball coach [Tim Vezie] who didn't want me to play baseball and the baseball coach [Jim Dietz] wasn't aware how much I loved the game," Gwynn said. "You want to give someone credit for getting the ball rolling, it

legend took wing. That was the day that Gwynn was drafted by both the San Diego Padres of the National League (third round) and the then-San Diego Clippers of the National Basketball Association (10th round).

Gwynn became the first athlete ever drafted by two different sports on the same day – a San Diego State athlete drafted by two San Diego professional teams.

"That pretty much tied me to San Diego," Gwynn said laughing a couple of years ago. "Even if I wanted to get out of here, I couldn't."

Over the years, Gwynn had chances to leave San Diego. All he had to do was let his contract run out and file for free agency. Certainly, bigger dollars were to be had elsewhere. His family knew it. His friends knew it. Gwynn knew it.

And Gwynn stayed – even late in his career, when his knees were failing. Several American League teams courted Gwynn as a designated hitter. Leaving might have extended his career.

But Gwynn stayed a Padre, even when his physical limitations forced him to the sidelines.

– Mr. San Diego –

"Looking back, this is where I fit," Gwynn said recently. "It is different here than other places. I could be Tony Gwynn in San Diego. This is where Alicia and I raised our family. This is where we built our life together. San Diego has been good for me. Besides, I'm an outfielder."

Tony Gwynn has been good for San Diego.

It is safe to ask where the Padres would have been without Tony Gwynn. Maybe they wouldn't even be in San Diego.

During his two decades as a Padre, Gwynn endured one major "fire sale" of talent, two ownership changes and at least two threats of the team's relocation. At least one general manager even discussed the possibility of trading away Gwynn.

"When you look at all the things that could have happened, it is amazing that a player in this age can remain with one team an entire career," Gwynn said. "It's not always the player who decides to leave."

Yes, there were highs.

As a Padre, Gwynn celebrated three NL West titles and made trips to the World Series in 1984 and 1998. And what San Diegan will ever forget his home run off David Wells in the first game of the 1998 World Series at Yankee Stadium?

On a more personal level, there are those 3,141 hits, record-tying eight NL batting championships,

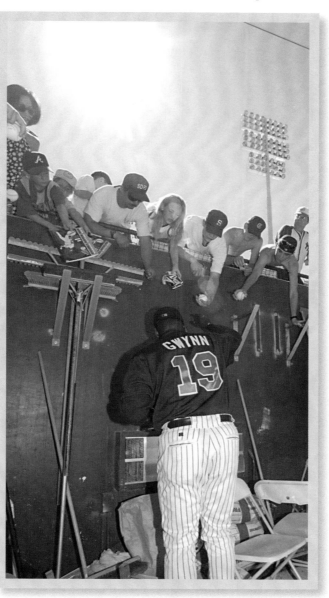

19 straight .300-plus seasons, 15 trips to the All-Star Game and five Gold Gloves.

In terms of baseball, Gwynn's influence extended well beyond San Diego.

With the help of wife Alicia, he was a pioneer in the use of videotape to study both hitting and pitchers. At first, Alicia taped Gwynn's at-bats off television. Then he lugged around his own equipment and hired his own video assistant. Today, every team employs a "video coach."

Much of Gwynn's impact is defined by his staggering numbers, figures that evoke awe and leave fans wondering "what if?"

What if the 1994 season hadn't ended by labor strife? Would Gwynn have become the first hitter since Ted Williams in 1941 to hit .400? He finished with a .394 mark – and to hear him tell it, he was just getting hot.

What if his knees didn't start disintegrating around his 30th birthday? Would Gwynn have made a run at Pete Rose's all-time hit record? Only once in his final 12 seasons did Gwynn approach 150 games. And in that 1997 season, Gwynn won his final batting title with a .372 mark and set career highs in hits (220), homers (17) and RBIs (119). Over his final four seasons, Gwynn averaged only 86 games and 275 at-bats per season.

– Mr. San Diego –

What if?

"I was a much better hitter at the end of my career than I was at the beginning," Gwynn said. "I adapted and learned. I am very proud of what I became as a hitter."

But his .338 career batting average is only a partial measure of Gwynn's value.

In San Diego, Gwynn has batted close to a thousand – on and off the field.

Gwynn was the smiling face of the Padres franchise in bad times as well as good. Fans turned off by everything else the perennial also-rans might be doing could always go to a game knowing Gwynn was there.

Even on those rare occasions when he didn't get a hit – and he got at least one in 76 percent of the games he started – he would give you a smile or an autograph.

"I'm a signing junkie," Gwynn once joked. "I had a collector once try to tell me how valuable my signature was going to be one day. Then he found out how much stuff I had signed over the years. He looked at me like the stock market had crashed."

Gwynn would spend time before almost every game signing for fans. But even there he had a soft spot.

"It's the little kid with a dirty T-shirt and dirty hands," Gwynn said. "I see a little dirty hand coming through the crush with a card and I'm all over it. It's the little kids who bring a smile to your face."

And Gwynn went out of his way to bring smiles to little kids' faces.

Beyond being a Hall of Fame player, Gwynn was a compassionate ambassador for the game as well as his team.

Again, the focus was on children. Early in his career, Tony and Alicia created a foundation that over the years supported a number of youth programs and organizations in the San Diego Community.

Gwynn was among the players who formed the Padres Scholars Program, which awards college scholarships annually to 25 middle school students, contingent upon their graduating from high school in good academic standing. The program has since been copied by other teams.

Much of Gwynn's work in the community is a matter of public record. But some of his and Alicia's most notable deeds are completed behind the scenes. For years, they have opened the doors to their personal home to troubled children.

In both 1997 and 1998, Gwynn was the Padres' nominee for the Roberto Clemente Man of the Year Award. In 1999, he was the national recipient of the honor. Gwynn has also won the Branch Rickey Award for outstanding community service by a major league player.

But Gwynn seemed to get as much joy out of packing up a box of used gloves, bats and balls for a struggling youth league as he did making a financial commitment.

"With kids, it's about time," Gwynn once said. "I wish I had more time."

Time, of course, is something that Gwynn is known for.

Tony Gwynn and fellow Hall of Fame inductee Cal Ripken Jr. are two of only 17 players in major league history to have played an entire career of 20 or more seasons with the same team.

"You can't do that and not create friendships that last a lifetime," Gwynn said.

Former Padres manager Bruce Bochy was first a

"VERY FEW ATHLETES HAVE HAD GREATER IMPACT ON THEIR COMMUNITY THAN TONY GWYNN."

– John Moores –

– Mr. San Diego –

teammate of Gwynn's and later managed him from 1995 through the end of his career.

"Tony is a rare athlete," Bochy said. "People around the game not only equate him with the Padres but with San Diego. I really don't know where the Padres would be had Tony not come along.

"To this day, he and [broadcaster] Jerry Coleman are the links to an earlier time ... to Ray Kroc, the World Series team of 1984. They are the bridge."

Gwynn's bridge still reaches the Padres.

He hasn't gone very far. After retiring as a player, Gwynn returned to his alma mater to succeed his college coach as San Diego State's baseball coach. He still drops by the television booth from time to time to be part of the Padres broadcast team.

On July 29, 2007, he will become the first lifetime Padre inducted into the Hall of Fame. And a statue of Gwynn will be unveiled outside Petco Park – which has the address of 19 Tony Gwynn Drive.

Connections.

It wasn't lost on Gwynn on the night of July 19, 1982. He had flown overnight from Hawaii (then the site of the Padres' Triple-A team) to join the Padres.

"Even then, I was thinking about coming home," Gwynn said years later. "That's how special it's going to be playing for the Padres after playing for San Diego State."

Gwynn's first major league hit that night was a double. But his most memorable hit was a ninth-inning single that put him at first base next to the game's all-time hit leader.

TONY GWYNN SPEAKS AT A NEWS CONFERENCE AT PETCO PARK ON JAN. 9, 2007, AFTER BEING VOTED INTO THE BASEBALL HALL OF FAME.

"I remember Pete Rose turning to me at the bag and joking with me not to catch him in one game," Gwynn said.

Well, Gwynn never did catch Rose. But 3,141 hits is a laudable total. He just wishes No. 3,000 came at a different site.

"Some things you can't [control] and getting my 3,000th on my mom's 64th birthday was special," Gwynn said. "But I wish it had happened in San Diego and not Montreal. I really wanted to do it before the fans who had supported me for so long. But you can't decide where and when things are going to happen."

Like where you play and for how long.

"San Diego has been special for me," Gwynn said. "There's a reason why it worked out like it did. I really believe that. It was meant for me to spend my entire career in San Diego.

"The city and the Padres have been good for Tony Gwynn." ☐

BILL CENTER HAS COVERED SPORTS FOR THE SAN DIEGO UNION-TRIBUNE SINCE 1967. HE FIRST MET TONY GWYNN IN 1978 AND HAS BEEN PART OF HIS NEWSPAPER'S PADRES COVERAGE TEAM SINCE 1982.

REPRESENTING TONY GWYNN

By | John Boggs

In the early 1980s, I was working for former Padre Steve Garvey at Garvey Marketing Group in San Diego. Garvey's locker was in the same row as Tony Gwynn's and, like many Padre fans, my relationship with Tony began with an admiration for what he did on the field.

As I began to get to know Tony and book appearances and marketing opportunities for him, I found out what every Padre fan in San Diego has learned, that he was both approachable and friendly. Tony's love and appreciation for the game of baseball were infectious and a pleasure to be around.

In 1985, my relationship with Tony took a major step forward as I booked him as a participant in the AT&T Baseball Challenge. A skills competition for major league players, the AT&T Baseball Challenge had a sizable prize for the winner and I felt Tony was a lock to win. Shortly after he secured a come-from-behind victory, fueled by his performance during the Home Run Derby, I began to represent Tony exclusively in his contracts and marketing.

In many ways our lives intersected at identical times; he was just beginning his career as a major leaguer and I was just starting my career as an agent. Tony's humility and dedication to his craft inspired me and helped me establish a framework and model for my business, an approach that I hold true today.

When I began representing Tony, he was already signed to a six-year deal with the Padres. One of the most challenging experiences of my career was trying to renegotiate and extend his contract to keep him in San Diego and ensure he was being paid fairly. Tony wanted to remain a Padre and fortunately, we managed to get deals done and keep Tony in San Diego for his entire career.

While I could write an entire book about experiences and memories with Tony, there are four memories which to me define Tony Gwynn, the ballplayer and the person.

Tony's work ethic as a hitter has been widely covered and deservedly so, but for me, Tony's dedication to his craft in the outfield was far more indicative of his character. Despite having a fielding percentage close to .990, he was perceived more as a hitter than a defensive player, but Tony sought to change that opinion. In 1986, Tony was awarded his first Gold Glove. I had the enormous pleasure of calling him while he was on vacation and giving him the great news. His reaction was priceless!

Establishing himself as one of the elite right fielders in the game, Tony won a second Gold Glove the following season and a total of five during his career.

One of my favorite memories of Tony, one that epitomized his abilities and mental toughness, was his

"WHAT BEGAN AS A PROFESSIONAL RELATIONSHIP HAS GROWN INTO ONE OF THE MOST REWARDING PERSONAL RELATIONSHIPS I HAVE EVER HAD."

– John Boggs –

– Representing Tony Gwynn –

race for the 1989 National League batting title against the San Francisco Giants' Will Clark. The two battled back and forth all season and the last three games of the year were in San Diego against the Giants. Heading into that series, Clark was hitting .333 and Tony was a tick below at .332. In the final two games of the series, Will went 2-for-8, maintaining his average of .333. Tony, on the other hand, delivered in a huge way. He went 6-for-8, clinching the batting title on the last day of the season. He knew he had to be nearly perfect and he was, successfully winning his fourth batting crown.

While most remember 1999 as the season Tony got his 3,000th hit, that season had a much more sentimental moment for me. The All-Star Game was held at Fenway Park for the first time in nearly 40 years. To honor the current All-Stars, along with those nominated for MasterCard's All-Century Team, All-Stars young and old, current and former gathered at Fenway.

In one of the most memorable moments in All-Star history, Ted Williams was driven to the pitcher's mound, where he was set to deliver the ceremonial first pitch of the evening. Waiting at the mound for him was Tony. Tony stood with Ted and supported his body so he could deliver the first pitch. In a moment that will forever be etched in my mind, Ted leaned into Tony and threw the pitch. This very public moment revealed to many the intimacy and depth of their friendship and mutual trust and respect, forever bringing Ted and Tony together in baseball history.

It was nearly a month later that Tony went on to achieve one of the most treasured milestones in

baseball, clubbing hit No. 3,000 on Aug. 6, 1999. I will never forget Tony's caravan of friends, family and fans traveling to St. Louis, where we anticipated his 3,000th hit. Then we had to scramble at the last minute and try to arrange transportation and accommodations so I could travel to Montreal, where Tony ultimately collected the magic hit. It was all worth it when he connected with that pitch and became a member of the 3,000-hit club.

Every agent dreams that their clients will have success on and off the field, but few can ever say that their first client became a Hall of Famer. From negotiating his contracts, booking commercial shoots or watching him attain baseball immortality, I have had the pleasure of representing Tony throughout his Hall of Fame career and I am thrilled to take that experience out into the field as I look for future Hall of Famers.

JOHN BOGGS CELEBRATES WITH TONY GWYNN FOLLOWING HIT NO. 3,000 IN MONTREAL.

What began as a professional relationship has grown into one of the most rewarding personal relationships I have ever had. Tony's contributions to the game, to the Padres and to San Diego have been a pleasure to watch and have inspired me on a daily basis.

Over the last 20 years, I have been behind Tony every step of the way and I will be with him in Cooperstown, watching him not only as my client, but also as his friend and a fan. □

WITH A BASE OF MORE THAN 50 CLIENTS, INCLUDING MORE THAN 15 CURRENT MAJOR LEAGUERS, AGENT JOHN BOGGS HAS EXCLUSIVELY REPRESENTED TONY GWYNN IN HIS CONTRACTS AND MARKETING FOR MORE THAN 20 YEARS. TO THIS DAY, THE SAN DIEGO-BASED BOGGS CREDITS GWYNN FOR HELPING HIM TO ESTABLISH HIS IDENTITY AND GIVING HIM THE CONFIDENCE TO BECOME A SUCCESSFUL AGENT.

COVERING TONY GWYNN

By | Jane Mitchell

In September 1996, the San Diego Padres and Cox Communications inked a deal to put 125-plus Padres games on television each year. I was hired to help create Channel 4 San Diego and to produce programming surrounding the team, namely the stories of the players. While a native San Diegan, I wasn't much of a sports fan. But I did know the name Tony Gwynn and it took me about five seconds of hearing him referred to as Mr. Padre to realize his place in the baseball landscape. So, of course, he was high on the list of people to profile for our new show, "One on One with Jane Mitchell."

I was scheduled to interview Tony the day before he would leave for spring training. While I felt confident in my own preparation, there was one thing I was a little nervous about – making sure the whole interview experience went well.

I had been told that Tony was the leader in the Padres' clubhouse. And if everything went well, I'd be in. But if it didn't, his opinion would carry clout. No pressure. Turns out, it did go well. I was prepared. And with lights, cameras and action at his kitchen table, he was willing to talk, and share, for nearly two hours.

The "One on One" telling of his life story – complete with pictures and interviews with his family

– debuted that June. That would be the real test. I'll never forget walking out to the field during batting practice a day or so after the show had first aired. Tony was sitting in the dugout. He called my name,

CHANNEL 4 SAN DIEGO'S JANE MITCHELL INTERVIEWS TONY GWYNN IN 1997 ...

then gave me a thumbs up. "Good job," he said. "Well done." I guess I was in.

While Tony could see I knew what I was doing from a television and show production standpoint, I was a rookie in the baseball world in 1997. And not to put words in his mouth, but I think Tony appreciated that I was trying to understand how it all worked. Never pretending to know more than I did. Never afraid to ask.

Tony, in the nicest of ways, was willing to teach me, too. The first time I was in the dugout area with a photographer

– Covering Tony Gwynn –

to shoot video, Tony pointed out to me where I could and could not stand. Essentially saying, "See that blue line? During the game, this side is our side. That side is your side. Stay there, and you'll be fine."

My first time traveling with the team, I'm sure I looked a little lost. Just trying to follow protocol. He nicely said to me, "You stay in the middle with the coaches and media. Don't go in the back with the players." And when we got back from the road trip, he checked in to make sure I got the traveling on the plane thing all figured out. I had. Thanks

Willie McCovey said he was "one of the greatest hitters of all time." Don Sutton said, "If it were possible to waive the five-year rule for Tony Gwynn, they would. He'll be here." Then, to read back those words to Tony and have him say, "Wow. That's nice. That's really nice. ... It's not my call. It's not my call."

Now, a decade later, producing three more "One on Ones" focused on Tony Gwynn ("Road to Cooperstown," "A Conversation with Tony Gwynn," and "Tony Gwynn at the Hall of Fame"), I feel honored that my work helps his fans connect with a humble, kind, talented man. These programs replay many times. So his story, his thoughts, his perspective are captured on video for his fans of all ages to see. Some who have known him far longer than I have. Some who are learning about him now, having never seen him play.

As I wrote at the conclusion of the "Road to Cooperstown" edition in April 2007: "These are exciting times for Tony Gwynn, his family, friends and his fans. Now, on a national stage, the rest of the baseball world will know what San Diegans have known for years. That he not only has quantifiable Hall of Fame numbers, but

... AND AGAIN IN 2007 AS HE PREPARES
TO ENTER THE HALL OF FAME.

to him. I was respectful of his world. He respected my role, too.

Never would I have imagined what my role with Channel 4 and my relationship with Tony Gwynn and his family would bring ... Traveling with the team as Tony was on the "Road to 3,000" ... Seeing the final hits in St. Louis and Montreal ... Being there the night he retired ... Having the pleasure of interviewing several Hall of Famers in 2001 (for Dave Winfield's induction) about Tony.

his character and charisma combine to make him a quality guy on his way to Cooperstown." □

JANE MITCHELL IS A 16-TIME EMMY AWARD WINNING JOURNALIST WHO HOSTS AND PRODUCES "ONE ON ONE WITH JANE MITCHELL" FOR CHANNEL 4 SAN DIEGO, THE SAN DIEGO PADRES' FLAGSHIP STATION. NOW IN ITS 11TH SEASON, "ONE ON ONE" GOES BEYOND THE BOXSCORES AND INTO THE HEARTS, SOULS AND SCRAPBOOKS OF SAN DIEGO'S SPORTS STARS, PAST, PRESENT AND FUTURE. TONY GWYNN HAS BEEN THE SUBJECT OF FIVE "ONE ON ONE" PROGRAMS: "TONY AND ALICIA GWYNN" (1997); "TONY GWYNN: CHAPTER 2" (2003); "TONY GWYNN'S ROAD TO COOPERSTOWN" (APRIL 2007); "A CONVERSATION WITH TONY GWYNN" (JULY 2007); AND "TONY GWYNN AT THE HALL OF FAME" (AUGUST 2007).

Less than 24 hours after his Hall of Fame career with the San Diego Padres ended, Tony Gwynn was in the batting cages at his college alma mater, working with walk-ons who had no clue what they were doing.

There was no time to decompress from his 20-year career, no plans for a cruise or even a golf vacation.

There was a new career to get ready for.

Two decades after he left San Diego State University, Gwynn was back, preparing to replace Jim Dietz, who had coached him years ago.

Once Gwynn made it known he wanted to replace Dietz, it was all but certain he was going to get the job. Really, how

meet Dietz.

"I said, 'Coach, I really would love the opportunity to play baseball.' Coach, he didn't explain anything, he just said, 'Oh yeah, sure, no problem.' So I came here thinking I was going to get the chance to play baseball, but as I found out later on, Coach had like 60, 70 walk-ons every year try out for the team."

On top of that, basketball coach Tim Vezie insisted that Gwynn concentrate on hoops that first year.

In the meantime, Dietz had recruited infielder Bobby Meacham, who knew Gwynn from summer ball in the Los Angeles area.

"So my sophomore year, Bobby tells Coach Dietz, 'Hey,

STUDENT TO TEACHER

By | B.J. Wilson

could the school say no to an eight-time National League batting champion and a member of the 3,000-hit club who also happened to be a distinguished alumnus?

"When I read in the paper [Dietz] was going to coach one more year and then he was going to retire, bells and whistles started going off in my head," Gwynn said. "I was playing still but I knew I was on my last leg.

"I kind of knew that this was going to be a one-time thing and if you want that job you need to get it. I came up here and said, 'Coach, would you be upset if I tried to get this job?' And he had a look on his face like, 'I knew you were going to be the one to want this job.' And we talked about it.

"I said, 'I don't want you to be upset. I hope you don't feel like I'm trying to run you out of here, but I kind of think that for my career path after baseball, this is the direction I want to go.' And he was all gung-ho about it. He said, 'You probably need to volunteer that last year because you can probably learn a lot.' And here I am."

Gwynn and Dietz have had a special relationship over the years, one that continues to this day. They first met when Gwynn was being courted by SDSU's basketball team. One of the assistant coaches brought him down to

you've got a pretty good baseball player on the basketball team,'" Gwynn said. "Coach Dietz says, 'Who?' Bobby says, 'Tony Gwynn. I played summer ball with him. That guy can play, man, you should bring him down here.'

"When basketball season ended, I came down here thinking that Coach Dietz already knew who I was and was going to give me an opportunity. I didn't know Bobby was the reason why he even gave me the chance, because Bobby told him I could play. So if Bobby Meacham doesn't come here, I'm nowhere on the radar screen."

Gwynn quickly found out that playing two sports wasn't as easy as it sounded.

"As it turned out, that first year, I sucked," Gwynn said with a hearty laugh. "It's a wonder Coach even saw anything in me. When you play basketball all year long and then come down here and play baseball, there was this animosity among the guys who've been here all year long. And so you have to deal with that and the only way you can deal with that is when you get the chance, be productive.

"The first year I hit .301, but it was an ugly .301. The next year when I got down here I was ready to go. I hit .420 or whatever and was a third team All-American. So the next year when I came down they were ready for me. They

– Student To Teacher –

knew I could play. But if it wasn't for Bobby Meacham, I wouldn't be sitting in this office right now."

Gwynn said Dietz was a disciplinarian and stressed fundamentals.

Gwynn said Dietz didn't tinker with his hitting, but he did help the outfielder improve his throwing.

"He really worked me on trying to throw, but it didn't really register until I started doing it every day," he said. "Remember, I played basketball from the end of baseball season all the way up until about March, then I'm playing baseball, like something to do on the side. So when I was coming down here, it was just like side action. I have to remember to throw, remember how to work my hands. By the time I really got good at it, the season was over.

"Coach Dietz was the one who said, 'If you do get the chance to play this at the next level, you really have to work at your craft because you're not as advanced as some of these other guys who've played all their lives. You're just playing it for three, four months at a time, and you really need to work at it.'

"So he was the one who gave me the insight into going about it the right way. When I signed, I knew I was just going to have to outwork everybody because they were way ahead of me."

And he did. Gwynn hit .398 during his SDSU career, with 102 RBIs, 18 homers, 35 stolen bases and 106 runs scored.

Sure enough, once he got to the big leagues, Gwynn was renowned for his work ethic. He worked on honing that sweet left-handed stroke and he popularized the use of video to study his at-bats.

"Granted he honed his craft once he got into professional ball, but for me he was a natural hitter at San Diego State," said former teammate Bud Black, now the Padres' manager. "He had the great ability to put the good part of the bat on the ball the majority of the time and the same type of hitter

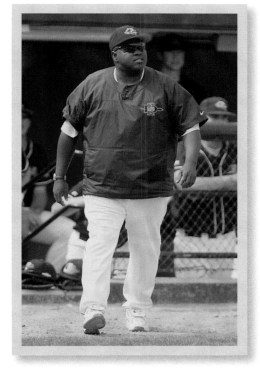

TWO DECADES AFTER HE LEFT SAN DIEGO STATE UNIVERSITY, TONY GWYNN RETURNED AS HIS ALMA MATER'S BASEBALL COACH.

– he sprayed the ball all over the field.

"The thing that I remember is he played with just a boyish enthusiasm. I'll always remember the laugh. He had the same laugh now as he had back then. He just loved being on the field. He's a cage rat, he's a gym rat. I just got the impression that he just loves sports. He's a sports nut."

Black and Meacham both remember how good Gwynn was back then.

"In high school or college, you can just tell who the players are and who aren't, who are going to advance. You just know it from the moment they walk on the field," Black said. "In Tony's case, the moment he walked on the field, right off the basketball court, we knew we had a player. To watch him through that season, we knew he was going to get an opportunity to play professional baseball, no doubt. It was shortly thereafter, just watching his short time in the minor leagues, we knew he was going to be a guy in the big leagues who could hit."

Said Meacham: "He wasn't just a great hitter. He was the best player I ever played with up until I got to the big leagues."

Meacham ended up playing for the New York Yankees, but he didn't come close to having the career Gwynn did.

"I always tease my son, 'Son, I was a first-rounder, he was a third-rounder. I was the MVP of that team,'" Meacham said. "I tell him, 'I was supposed to be good, son.'"

Fast forward 26 years, and Gwynn is basking in the glow of a Hall of Fame election while still trying to get the Aztecs to the regionals.

Gwynn said his election validates his style of hitting. He said his first-ballot election was a victory for the little guy, someone who made a career out of hitting singles and doubles into the gaps, rather than driving the ball over the fence.

"I knew who I was," he said. "I was comfortable with who I was. I'm excited about it because it gives me an opportunity

– Student To Teacher –

to toot the horn of the contact guy, that guy who doesn't hit a whole lot of home runs, who sprays singles and doubles all around the yard, gets on base and scores runs. That's basically what I did."

Cal Ripken Jr. got 537 votes and appeared on 98.53 percent of ballots to finish with the third-highest percentage ever behind Tom Seaver (98.84) and Nolan Ryan (98.79).

Gwynn received 532 votes for a 97.61 percent, the seventh-highest.

"Validation. That's the word I keep going back to," Gwynn said. "Because for a hitter like me, I needed to do a lot of what I did to have a chance. I got my chance. I was a good player. I knew my place. I was not a game-changer; I was not a dominant guy."

The left-handed hitter won eight batting titles to tie Honus Wagner's NL record, finishing with 3,141 hits and a .338 career average. He made 15 All-Star teams, won five Gold Gloves as an outfielder and helped the Padres reach the World Series twice, where they lost to the Detroit Tigers in 1984 and the New York Yankees in 1998.

Upon retirement, Padres owner John Moores presented Gwynn with a sports utility vehicle.

"For those of us who expect to live forever, we're never going to see a day like this in the history of the franchise," Moores said.

Gwynn looks back at his playing days at SDSU and is glad he persisted in playing baseball. He was good enough as the school's point guard to be drafted in the 10th round by the San Diego Clippers in 1981, on the same day that the Padres took him in the third round.

Gwynn figures he could have played a year or so in the NBA.

"I had played baseball my whole life but never really concentrated on it," he said. "And I knew that if I was going to make it professionally, this was going to be my best shot."

"It was a nice gesture," said Gwynn about getting drafted by the Clippers. "But I knew where I needed to go. I knew in my own mind I could play big league ball. You just didn't know when the opportunity was going to present itself."

Gwynn retired following the 2001 season, then got right to work on Montezuma Mesa. He's glad now that he spent that one season as a volunteer coach before succeeding Dietz.

"I learned a lot and then I got the job and then I even learned a whole lot more because when you're the head guy, there are a whole lot of things you don't really think about that you've got to deal with, and it's great," he said. "It's time consuming, it's a roll-up-the-sleeves kind of job. You've got to do some politicking and you've got to do some hobnobbing, but I like it."

Gwynn and Dietz still talk, and sometimes they disagree. Gwynn likes to play a tough schedule, but Dietz has suggested the Aztecs play an easier one.

"The biggest thing he helped me with was structure," Gwynn said. "You've got to have structure to what you do. And when I got here I didn't have it and it showed on the field. I've been fortunate because I've had some pretty good teams here and we've had some success here, but not the kind of consistent success that Coach had."

Gwynn recalls that Dietz started every practice with the same drills. Although that might have been boring for the players, Gwynn now sees its importance.

He also recalls Dietz having 18 signs. When Dietz missed five games with illness during his final season, Gwynn took over and cut the signs to three – bunt, hit and run and steal.

"We rattled off four in a row," Gwynn said. "That kind of made me think it was going to be easy. All I did was simplify signs. Coach went back to 18 signs. I didn't think we needed that many. He told me, 'It was too simple. You have to make kids think. You have to make them work.'"

Now, Gwynn will only say that he has more than three signs but fewer than 18.

> G
>
> "MORE THAN ANYTHING, YOUR GUYS NEED TO SEE YOU HAVE PASSION FOR WHAT YOU'RE DOING."
>
> – Tony Gwynn –

– Student To Teacher –

"Again, I came in here thinking it was going to be easy," Gwynn said. "So I just felt like that was going to be an easier way for guys to get what we were talking about. What I found out was it was the complete opposite. You need to give guys lots to think about because it forces them to concentrate. I wouldn't do anything different. I think you have to bump your head before you realize that things are never as easy as you think they are."

Gwynn tries to copy his mentor in another way.

"More than anything, your guys need to see you have passion for what you're doing," he said. "They've got to see that you truly enjoy doing what you're doing. When I was playing, you could see that in Coach because he wanted the best for us. You can't help but learn from that and that's what we try to pass on to these kids now."

Dietz thinks Gwynn is doing a good job as a coach.

Winning certainly hasn't come as easily as Gwynn thought when he succeeded Dietz. He entered this, his fifth season, with a record of 113-132.

"I'm tired of losing," he said. "I'm alumni, too. Coach Dietz did a super job here, took the team to regionals and all that, and we haven't been able to crack that barrier. College baseball is at a point now where it's getting more attention than it's ever gotten. You've either got to keep up or you'll be looking for a new job. It's just that simple."

Gwynn said he's not feeling heat from his boss, but it irks him that the Aztecs haven't been able to win despite playing in a city full of prep talent. The Aztecs have never made it to the College World Series. They haven't been to the regionals since 1991.

After going 23-36 last year and making a quick exit from the Mountain West Conference Tournament, Gwynn completely changed the makeup of his squad. He loaded up on pitching in hopes of not hitting the wall in the conference tournament, like the Aztecs have in the past.

JIM DIETZ SPENT 31 YEARS AT SAN DIEGO STATE UNIVERSITY BEFORE RETIRING IN 2002.

Without a history of winning, recruiting is challenging for the Aztecs and Gwynn. He has found that many recruits just want the famous coach to visit their home, then they decide to go elsewhere.

"It's just gotten so competitive out there that a lot of kids who grew up playing baseball here don't want to stay here," Gwynn said. "They want to go somewhere else, want to go to programs where they have winning traditions. I think we do too, but we haven't won in a long time. For us to kind of scale this mountain that we're trying to climb, we need to win. It's just that simple. If you win, it changes everything."

Even before he became the Aztecs' coach, Gwynn was honored with the building of Tony Gwynn Stadium, a cozy little ballpark that was paid for mostly with a donation from Moores.

Gwynn doesn't like the attention it draws, but it's certainly a sweet place to play.

"I've gotten used to it," Gwynn said. "I still don't like it, because when you're an Aztec there are so many people here who have helped this program get to where it is. To single me out to be that guy, that signature guy, is kind of unfair to all those other people and I told John this when he built the ballpark and I have to go back to his answer, which was, 'Do you want the ballpark or not?' That's why it is what it is."

Gwynn did restore the name of Charlie Smith Field, which is what it was originally called. Smith was the Aztecs' coach from 1936-64.

"I think that's how it should be, Charlie Smith Field at Tony Gwynn Stadium," Gwynn said. "I just say 'Smith Field,' or I just say the ballpark. It's weird to see these schedules come out and where is it at? It's at Tony Gwynn Stadium. You kind of get used to it, but I still don't feel comfortable with it." ☐

B.J. WILSON COVERED THE SECOND HALF OF TONY GWYNN'S CAREER WITH THE PADRES.

PressBox | Tony, where does your election to the Hall of Fame stand in your long list of accomplishments?

Tony Gwynn | Right at the top. When you start out playing, this is the last thing you think of. It's at the top of the list. You don't think of this when you start playing, but as your career is winding down. … It's really been unbelievable. The ride thus far has been great … and it's going to get even more unbelievable. People say your life changes, and it really does. People know who you are. It's confirmation that you left your mark.

- - - - - - - -

PB | Both you and your fellow Hall of Fame electee this year, Cal Ripken Jr., played your entire careers in one city with one

TG | Well, there were lots of guys. Bobby Tolan was one. He made me believe that what I was doing could work. … The major leaguers were on strike the year I got drafted and when they shipped me off to Walla Walla (Wash.), I had never, at that point, really worked at the game. I'd practiced the game, but I'd never really worked at it because I had played basketball in high school and college. Every time I would come out for baseball, the season had already started. When I signed in '81, they shipped me off to Walla Walla and the major leaguers were on strike. Bobby Tolan was the first hitting guy that I had dealt with that really kind of broke it down for me and explained to me my type of swing and the

Q&A WITH MR. PADRE

team. What did that mean to you and what might that signify to people when they look at the totality of your career?

TG | For me, it was kind of important, I thought, because obviously that's where I started out and it was the perfect place for a whole lot of time spent doing stuff other than preparing for baseball. I learned early on in my career that being in the middle of the country, being on the East Coast, there's a lot more responsibilities than out here on the West Coast. And I kind of liked that. I liked working my craft, doing my thing. And yeah, we had media here that we had to deal with. I had plenty of time to really work at my craft. When I was a guy starting out, I needed to. I really had to work to get better. The fact that I ended up playing all 20 years with the Padres was very important to me because it meant I was wanted. And growing up as a Dodgers fan in L.A. or in Long Beach, I saw a Dodgers infield that played together for eight years. As a fan, I loved that. I loved knowing that they were going to be out there every day. I'm sure there were other people in this town that felt that way. It takes a lot of luck; I'm not going to lie. Obviously, you need to be protective, but you also need to be wanted.

- - - - - - - -

PB | Prior to arriving in the majors, who was the most influential person in your development as a baseball player?

things I needed to do. He was very influential early in my professional career.

- - - - - - - -

PB | Who was the most significant person in your career once you got to the big leagues?

TG | I would say Dick Williams because he set the foundation for what type of player I was going to be. Dick was no nonsense. You learned to do it the right way; he wanted you to prepare and he didn't like excuses. He was a "get the job done" type of man. I played for him my first two years in the big leagues. I owe a lot to him because I didn't want to make mistakes. When I made them, he would let me know I made them, but then I would learn from them and got better. So I would say Dick Williams, but again, there's so many people that had a hand in me becoming who I became. It would be unfair to just single one person out.

Bobby Tolan when I first got to pro ball, and then Dick Williams when I got to the big leagues, but then there were other guys. Larry Bowa – he just had so much passion for the game that it just rubbed off on me. He was our manager, but he just had passion, man. I know that if he could put a uniform on, if he could go out there with us, he would've wanted to be out there. That rubs off on you. You might not like his style. You might not like the fact that he has a temper,

1983

1984

1985

1986

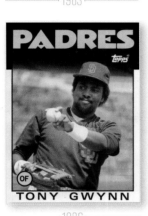

1986

1987

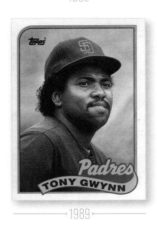

1989

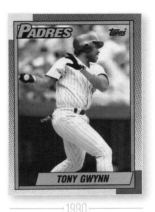

1990

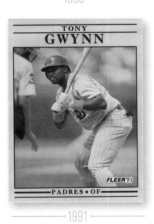

1991

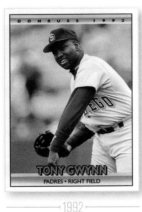

1992

1992

1993

1994

1996

1998

1999

BY THE NUMBERS

9,288 Career at-bats for Tony Gwynn

3,141 Career hits for Tony Gwynn

434 Career strikeouts for Tony Gwynn

.338 Lifetime batting average of Tony Gwynn

8 Batting titles won by Tony Gwynn:
1984 (.351)	1987 (.370)
1988 (.313)	1989 (.336)
1994 (.394)	1995 (.368)
1996 (.353)	1997 (.372)

4 Numbers retired by the Padres, including Tony Gwynn's No. 19, which was retired by the Padres on Sept. 4, 2004:
6 - Steve Garvey	19 - Tony Gwynn
31 - Dave Winfield	35 - Randy Jones

TONY GWYNN CONNECTS FOR HIT NO. 3,000 AGAINST THE EXPOS IN MONTREAL ON AUG. 6, 1999.